Moodle 1.9 Theme Design
Beginner's Guide

Customize the appearance of your Moodle Theme by using
Moodle's powerful theming engine

Paul James Gadsdon

BIRMINGHAM - MUMBAI

Moodle 1.9 Theme Design
Beginner's Guide

First published: April 2010

Production Reference: 1150410

Published by Packt Publishing Ltd.
32 Lincoln Road
Olton
Birmingham, B27 6PA, UK.

ISBN 978-1-849510-14-1

www.packtpub.com

Cover Image by Ed Maclean (edmaclean@gmail.com)

Credits

Author

Paul James Gadsdon

Reviewer

Mauno Korpelainen

Acquisition Editor

David Barnes

Development Editor

Dhiraj Chandiramani

Technical Editor

Namita Sahni

Copy Editor

Lakshmi Menon

Indexer

Hemangini Bari

Editorial Team Leader

Akshara Aware

Project Team Leader

Priya Mukherji

Project Coordinator

Prasad Rai

Proofreaders

Joel T. Johnson

Dirk Manuel

Graphics

Geetanjali Sawant

Production Coordinator

Aparna Bhagat

Cover Work

Aparna Bhagat

About the Author

Paul James Gadsdon has been at the forefront of the web development industry for more than 12 years. He has worked as a web developer/designer and project manager for various national and international companies during this period. He has also worked for a local government in an advisory capacity, and undertakes consultancy work in a variety of technical subjects. His technical expertise lies in areas such as SQL, ASP, ASP.Net, VB, C#, DotNetNuke, Joomla, and PHP. Some four years ago he became involved in Moodle and since then he has worked as an e-Learning Technologist and a Moodle Virtual Learning Environment Developer.

Paul currently works for the University of Wales, Lampeter.

I would like to thank my partner Steph Copson for the whole 30 minutes of patience she afforded me over the time of writing this book.

About the Reviewer

Mauno Korpelainen teaches Mathematics for high school and adult students in Hyvinkää, Finland and has been a PHM (Particularly Helpful Moodler) for several years, and is one of the moderators of the `moodle.org` forums.

Table of Contents

Preface

Moodle—Modular Object-Oriented Dynamic Learning Environment—is a free, open source e-learning platform. It is one of the most popular Virtual Learning Environments (VLEs) available today, and is used as a teaching and learning tool in schools, colleges, universities, and more recently in the corporate environment.

The proliferation of Moodle for learning and teaching means that there has never been a better time to become familiar with this e-learning platform. This book focuses on the visual customization (theming) of Moodle so that Moodle can be customized to match your educational institution's or corporate branding guidelines. It will guide you step by step through the processes required to create your own Moodle theme while helping to ensure that you understand what might be required of your theme in terms of web standards and browser compatibility.

This book is split into two sections:

Section 1, *Getting Started* (Chapters 01 to 05), helps you become familiar with Moodle themes and how to customize themes by using HTML (Hypertext Markup Language) and CSS (Cascading Style Sheets).

Section 2, *Creating a standards-compatible, accessible Moodle theme*, shows you how to create a Moodle theme from scratch. It shows you how to visualize your planned theme and turn this concept into a fully-compatible, working Moodle theme.

What this book covers

Chapter 1, An Introduction to Moodle, introduces you to Moodle, explaining what Moodle is and how it works. It will also cover why Moodle should be used. You compare Moodle to other Course Management Systems (CMSes) and Virtual Learning Environments (VLEs) and this chapter details Moodle's pedagogic principles. This chapter also outlines why the book has been written and who its intended audience is. Finally, it discusses what software and hardware tools you will need, and makes some assumptions with regards to the ICT and web design/development skills needed to complete this book.

Chapter 2, Moodle Themes, covers the basics of Moodle theming, including theme types, priority, location of the theme directory, and the concept of parent themes. We also cover browsing and changing a theme within Moodle, and also searching for, downloading, and installing custom themes. We then finish off by changing the theme settings on the Moodle theme settings page.

Chapter 3, Customizing the Header and Footer, covers the steps needed to make changes to the `header.html` and `footer.html` files in the `theme` directory of your Moodle site. You start by making some small changes, such as changing the logo and the title text so that you can see how easy it is to customize the header in Moodle. This chapter also looks at some basic HTML recommendations to keep your Moodle theme standards-compliant. Then it moves on to changing the footer, including or removing the Moodle logo and login info links, and adding your own copyright or footer text. Finally, in this chapter, you learn to check that your changes are standards-compliant and look similar in more than one web browser.

Chapter 4, Adjusting the Colors and Fonts, initially covers what Cascading Style Sheets are, and why stylesheets are important when theming Moodle. After this, you learn to change the default font, set the font size and color, set the link color, and change the background color by using CSS. Additionally, this chapter focuses on the concept of "accessibility" so that you can theme Moodle with accessibility in mind from the outset.

Chapter 5, Changing the Layout, teaches you how to change the default layout of Moodle through the use of CSS. It covers setting the width of the Moodle site and you learn to understand the differences between fixed and liquid Moodle theme designs. You then move on to learn how to change the width of the sideblocks and introduce resolution-independent design concepts while you work through the exercises.

Chapter 6, Planning your Moodle Theme, introduces the concept of "know your audience" and continues with this by making sure that you create your own goals for your Moodle theme before continuing with the "planning and gathering assets" stage. In this section, you learn about the need to think about the images or graphics that might be needed and also to decide whether animation or static graphics should be used. Informal research is the key to this stage. This chapter then addresses how you should create the design for the

Moodle theme, from a simple paper mockup to a full-blown exact copy built using a graphics software application (a mockup).

Chapter 7, First Steps: Creating your First Complete Moodle Theme, starts the process of creating your first complete Moodle theme. You learn a little more about themes, parent themes, and how to set these in Moodle's configuration files.

Chapter 8, Creating your Moodle theme from your Mockup: Slice and Dice, helps you start to "slice and dice", taking you through a series of exercises so that you can edit the header and footer of your Moodle theme to match that of the mockup that you created in the planning stage. This chapter also takes you through the process of changing all of the links, fonts, headings, and background, and continues on to changing the themes' icons and testing the changes that you have made.

Chapter 9, Under the Hood: Style your Navigation, Login Screen, and Blocks, further develops your skills learned in Chapter 8 to show you how to change the look and feel of some more functional elements of Moodle. This includes elements such as the splash page login screen, the width and appearance of the sideblock headers and sideblock content areas. You also learn how to style the breadcrumb trail and test these changes in multiple browsers.

Chapter 10, Under the Hood: Theming Core Functionality and Modules, allows you to change the appearance of some of the core code (non-contributed) parts of Moodle. You first look at theming the central content part of your Moodle site, including the home page course category pages and the actual course view. You then move on to learn how to theme the forum and glossary modules to match your theme. You change only a small amount in each module so that you can pave the way to further improvements, in the next chapter.

Appendix A, Further Enhancements, elaborates some further enhancements that you can make to your new theme and ways by which you can test that all of the functionality within Moodle works the way that it is supposed to. We discuss ways by which we can streamline some of the actions that we have been undertaking, such as grouping CSS styles. You also correct a few problems that the author has noticed and create rollover and drop-down menus, among other things.

Appendix B, Glossary of Useful Terms and Acronyms, is a simple glossary of the terms, definitions, and acronyms that you will come across while learning about Moodle and Moodle themes.

Appendix C, Pop Quiz Answers, contains the answers to the pop quizzes.

Who this book is for

If you are a Moodle administrator, ICT technical personnel, designer, or a teacher, and wish to enhance your Moodle site to make it visually attractive, then this book is for you. You should be familiar with the basics of Moodle operation, and some familiarity with web design techniques, such as HTML and CSS, will be helpful.

Conventions

In this book, you will find several headings appearing frequently.

To give clear instructions of how to complete a procedure or task, we use:

Time for action – heading

1. Action 1

2. Action 2

3. Action 3

Instructions often need some extra explanation so that they make sense, so they are followed with:

What just happened?

This heading explains the working of tasks or instructions that you have just completed.

You will also find some other learning aids in the book, including:

Pop quiz – heading

These are short multiple choice questions intended to help you test your own understanding.

Have a go hero – heading

These sections set practical challenges and give you ideas for experimenting with what you have learned.

You will also find a number of styles of text that distinguish between different kinds of information. Here are some examples of these styles and an explanation of their meaning.

Code words in text are shown as follows: "We can include other contexts through the use of the `include` directive."

A block of code is set as follows:

```php
<?php print_container_start(true, '', 'header-home'); ?>
  <h1 class="headermain"><?php echo $heading ?></h1>
  <div class="headermenu"><?php echo $menu ?></div>
<?php print_container_end(); ?>
```

When we wish to draw your attention to a particular part of a code block, the relevant lines or items are set in bold:

```php
<?php print_container_start(true, '', 'header-home'); ?>
  <h1 class="headermain">
    <img src="<?php echo $CFG->themewww .'/'.
    current_theme() ?>/pix/logo.gif" alt="" />
  <?php echo $heading ?></h1>
  <div class="headermenu"><?php echo $menu ?></div>
<?php print_container_end(); ?>
```

New terms and **important words** are shown in bold. Words that you see on the screen, in menus or dialog boxes for example, appear in the text like this: " Click on **Run** and wait for the **Mozilla Firefox Setup Wizard** to appear ".

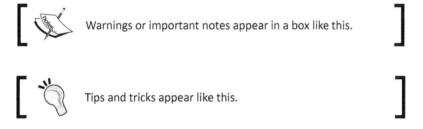

Warnings or important notes appear in a box like this.

Tips and tricks appear like this.

Reader feedback

Feedback from our readers is always welcome. Let us know what you think about this book—what you liked or may have disliked. Reader feedback is important for us to develop titles that you really get the most out of.

To send us general feedback, simply send an e-mail to feedback@packtpub.com, and mention the book title in the subject of your message.

If there is a book that you need and would like to see us publish, please send us a note via the **SUGGEST A TITLE** form on www.packtpub.com, or e-mail suggest@packtpub.com.

If there is a topic that you have expertise in and you are interested in either writing or contributing to a book on, see our author guide at www.packtpub.com/authors.

Customer support

Now that you are the proud owner of a Packt book, we have a number of things to help you to get the most from your purchase.

> **Downloading the example code for the book**
>
> Visit `http://www.packtpub.com/files/code/0141_Code.zip` to directly download the example code.
>
> The downloadable files contain instructions on how to use them.

Errata

Although we have taken every care to ensure the accuracy of our content, mistakes do happen. If you find a mistake in one of our books—maybe a mistake in the text or the code—we would be grateful if you would report this to us. By doing so, you can save other readers from frustration and help us to improve subsequent versions of this book. If you find any errata, please report them by visiting `http://www.packtpub.com/support`, selecting your book, clicking on the **let us know** link, and entering the details of your errata. Once your errata are verified, your submission will be accepted and the errata will be uploaded on our website, or added to any list of existing errata, under the Errata section of that title. Any existing errata can be viewed by selecting your title from `http://www.packtpub.com/support`.

Piracy

Piracy of copyright material on the Internet is an ongoing problem across all media. At Packt, we take the protection of our copyright and licenses very seriously. If you come across any illegal copies of our works, in any form, on the Internet, please provide us with the location address or website name immediately so that we can pursue a remedy.

Please contact us at `copyright@packtpub.com` with a link to the suspected pirated material.

We appreciate your help in protecting our authors and our ability to bring you valuable content.

Questions

You can contact us at `questions@packtpub.com` if you are having a problem with any aspect of the book, and we will do our best to address it.

1
An Introduction to Moodle

Chapter 1 introduces Moodle, explaining what Moodle is and how it works. It will also cover why Moodle should be used. It is compared to other Course Management Systems (CMS) and Virtual Learning Environments (VLEs) and it details Moodle's pedagogic principles. This chapter also outlines why the book has been written and who its intended audience is. Finally, it discusses what software and hardware tools you will need, and makes some assumptions with regards to the ICT and web design/development skills needed to get the most from this book.

In this chapter, we shall cover:

- What a Virtual Leaning Environment (VLE) is
- What types of VLE there are
- What are the advantages of using a VLE
- What Moodle is
- Why we should use Moodle
- What we will be doing in the rest of this book
- What skills we will need
- What tools we will need

If you teach or are involved in information technology for an educational institution, you will have probably heard the terms **Course Management Systems (CMS)**, **Learning Management Systems (LMS)**, and **Virtual Learning Environments (VLEs)**. These three terms can effectively be grouped into one and for the purposes of this book—you will refer to them as VLEs. Ever since the beginning of the Internet, there were promises that technology would transform the way by which education and learning takes place. However, this didn't happen straightaway. Rather, these transformations have evolved slowly over time, and this evolution in the way in which teaching and learning takes place is only now finally being realized.

What are Virtual Learning Environments?

Virtual Learning Environments normally consist of a number of files and a database, and are run online over the Internet. Most VLEs are completely web browser-based, meaning that people can access them anywhere provided they have an active Internet connection and suitable web browsing software.

VLEs are software systems designed to support teaching and learning in an educational environment.

The idea behind VLEs is that they provide access to learner resources and can be used to provide an enhanced learner experience and therefore supplement traditional learner resources such as classroom-based teaching and tutorials. They facilitate online interaction between students and teachers, and provide a method by which distance learners can access course materials.

The functions and activities supported by VLEs differ across different VLE software packages, but most include at least some of the following:

- Importing/exporting and/or creation of course materials
- Delivery of course materials over the Internet
- Communication and collaboration between students and educators
- Online tracking and assessment of student progress
- Modularized activities and resources
- Customization of the interface

Let's have a quick look at each of these functions and see how they might be useful.

Importing/exporting and/or creation of course materials

Most VLEs provide a set of tools that allow the import and export of course materials. These course materials might have already been created by using other standardized e-learning packages or software and therefore can be imported and exported in specific formats. This is very useful for educators, as it allows for the creation of a standardized package that course materials can reside in. So, whether the educational institution uses Moodle, WebCT, Blackboard, or any other VLE, course material can usually be migrated between these platforms.

The creation of course materials enables the educator to design their courses to fit an online environment. Course materials can either be created through the use of online forms or can be uploaded in a variety of formats such as Word or PDF. Courses can also be structured in a variety of ways, such as weekly or by topics, so that educators are not bound by normal academic terms.

Delivery of course materials over the Internet

One of the beneficial features of a VLE is that VLEs are available over the Internet or the institution's intranet. So users of these systems can access their learner materials anywhere there is an active Internet or intranet connection. This is hugely beneficial, as learners can use the VLE when and where they want. This functionality has particular relevance to distance learners who traditionally only received an education pack to supplement their studies.

VLEs are normally protected through a login system that doesn't allow the general public access to the learner materials and therefore can help to protect the intellectual property rights of the learner materials. VLEs also provide access for the educators to add or create these materials from any active Internet connection, which can reduce the need for educators to be present all of the time at their workplace.

Communication and collaboration between students and educators

Communication and **collaboration** are the latest terms that people use when referring to VLEs and the benefits of using them. One of the key principles behind most VLEs is that they allow communication channels between students, and between students and teachers, to open up. Student communication—especially with distance learners—can provide additional learner resources and can help the students to construct knowledge to an extent that they might not have been able to without these new technologies. Distance learners, for instance, can often feel very isolated and sometimes struggle to understand concepts because they haven't had the opportunity to discuss these with other students.

VLEs use a variety of features that take advantage of the communication aspects of education, from online forums and chats, to blogs and even wikis.

This type of communication and collaboration is often referred to as Web 2.0, and is based on information-sharing applications and concepts such as social networking. VLEs are now moving towards this end insofar as they are starting to embrace the concept of communication in these ways.

Online tracking and assessment of student progress

Most VLEs have the ability to allow educators to track the progress of students and grade their work as they study. There are a variety of ways in which this can be done, from the grading of assessed work that is submitted to the VLE to simple quizzes and questionnaires that allow the educators to gauge students' comprehension of the materials and to check the students' progress through the course by less formal methods.

Modularized activities and resources

Many VLEs provide modularized activities and resources so that the educator can create course materials the way they would like to, and also pick what functionality best suits their educational environment.

Customization of the interface

VLEs normally provide the ability to customize their interface so that institutions can develop the look and feel that they require, or create a site that matches their institution's branding. Customization is a very important element of the functionality of a VLE, otherwise all VLE sites would look the same. This has particular relevance to this book, as you will later be learning how to customize Moodle in terms of its look and feel.

What types of VLEs are there?

There are a number of established companies producing what are, for the purpose of this book, called Virtual Learning Environments. There are also a few emerging commercial brands and some open source alternatives that are gathering recognition in the education sector. WebCT and Blackboard are probably the most well known of the commercial products, and Moodle is the best known free, open source alternative.

In most cases, you will find that the term Virtual Learning Environments can be used interchangeably with other terms such as **Managed Learning Environments (MLE)**, **Course Management Systems (CMS)**, **Learning Support System (LSS)**, **Learning Platform (LP)**, and **Learning Management Systems (LMS)**. Although I prefer to keep it like that to makes things easier, there are subtle differences between these systems.

The one that really is different is an MLE, which is a system that is used to manage all of the ICT systems of an institution relating to the students' education, such as the student records MIS system and the VLE. So in these terms, a VLE or CMS would be a part of an MLE, being that the MLE manages all of the related student records and educations systems.

What are the advantages of using a VLE?

This is the big question and requires your organization to consider it in an objective manner. After all, we have been educating people for hundreds of years without the use of computers and the Internet. Classroom teaching is still the predominant method used in the education of people and will probably remain so for quite a number of years. However, VLEs can be an excellent way of supplementing traditional classroom teaching methods, and can also be used effectively as standalone teaching environments for distance learners. They offer a simple, streamlined method by which educators can create and publish educational materials and subsequently, offer a more accessible means by which learners can access learning materials.

VLEs provide timely access to learning materials and can supplement traditional teaching methods. They provide a platform for educators and support personnel to manage and execute all of their normal daily tasks including:

◆ Student cohort administration, organization, and the management of learner contact channels

◆ Assessment and monitoring of learners

◆ The creation of structured learning content by using existing teaching materials

◆ Management of student assessment and grades in one central place

◆ Reduction of learner resources such as printing and photocopying

VLEs also provide a platform for learners and give them timely access to the learning resources and support their learning both in the classroom and at home. For example:

◆ Students can submit their assignments online and track their progress over the course or degree programme.

◆ VLEs normally promote collaboration and communication between learners and educators.

◆ Students can choose to learn at their own pace. This is useful for accommodating any special needs of the students and distance learners.

What is Moodle?

Moodle is an open source software package that is used to create Internet-based learning materials and courses. Moodle is provided freely under the open source GNU Public License. This means that Moodle is copyrighted, but the users have the right to copy, use, and modify the source code provided that they agree to provide the modified source to others, do not remove or modify the original license and copyrights, and apply the same license to any derivative work. This, in layman's terms, means that you can do what you like to Moodle as long as you ensure that you do not attempt to copyright any of the modifications that you might introduce.

Moodle was originally an acronym for **Modular Oriented Dynamic Learning Environment**, which of course is mouthful and not very useful unless you are an educational theorist. At the time of writing, Moodle has a significant user base of some 43,000 registered sites in 208 countries, and is continuing to grow at a significant rate.

Moodle can be installed and run on any web server software that uses **Hypertext Preprocessor** (**PHP**), and can support a SQL database. MySQL is the database of choice, but Moodle can nevertheless be run on MS SQL, Oracle, and most other types of SQL databases.

Moodle can be run on the Windows and Apple Mac operating systems, and can also be installed on many different Linux distributions, including Red Hat, Ubuntu, and CentOS.

Moodle has many features that are expected from most e-learning platforms, and also has some of its own innovative features that set it aside. Moodle is a modular platform and therefore can be built to order, and can be readily extended through the use of third-party modules and extensions.

Why should I use Moodle?

Why should you use Moodle over any other VLE? The problem here normally lies in the fact that people are often wedded to what they are already using and therefore prefer to remain using the VLE software that the organization has decided to use. Either that, or they just prefer traditional classroom teaching methods.

There are a large number of commercial and free open source VLEs currently in the market, all of which offer a basic feature set with some extra features that normally set them apart from other VLEs. Moodle, however, seems to have the most features straight out of the box and is therefore seen as the benchmark against which other VLEs have to judge themselves.

Features

Moodle's features compare quite favorably against the other heavyweight, commercial VLEs insofar as over the last few years it has been Blackboard and WebCT's job to catch up on the feature list. Blackboard, for instance, has only recently had student peer review and HTML content creation functionally added to its feature set, whereas Moodle has had these features for a number of years.

Philosophy

Moodle has been designed to help educators create online learning materials and has been designed to support a social constructionist framework for education, insofar as its pedagogy follows the theory that groups of students or cohorts construct knowledge from one another in a collaborative way. So Moodle therefore supports communication and collaboration between students, groups of students, and tutors.

Community

The support channels for Moodle are second to none, and are based on the open source philosophy. This means that there are a lot more support channels that can be accessed than with commercial software VLEs. For instance, there is a very large resource available on `Moodle.org` called **Moodle** docs. This has been based on a wiki engine and has been built through the hard work of the Moodle community. This is a huge resource and is far larger than any commercial VLE software could ever possibly create as it's been created by thousands of Moodle users. Moodle docs can be found at `http://moodle.org/docs`.

There are also community forums on `Moodle.org`, which are accessed by tens of thousands of Moodle experts on a daily basis to get and give expert advice on every aspect of Moodle.

However, if an organization needs more timely support, then there are also a large number of commercial Moodle support companies (Moodle partners) that can offer paid support contracts and service level agreements. And as `Moodle.org` suggests on its website, this creates an environment of competition, thereby leading to lower prices, more choice, and better service.

Free and open source

Moodle is free, or is it? The open source movement often likes to use the *free* part of the title in order to immediately convince people that this has to be the way forward. It must be noted here that nothing is free—it might just be cheaper than a comparable commercial product. For instance, the total cost of ownership for Moodle is relatively low but it is not zero, or free in any way. Okay, Moodle is free to download and install and there aren't any application software licenses to purchase. However, in order for an organization to use Moodle, they will need to purchase the ICT infrastructure and either purchase a support contract or employ a Moodle administrator. And in my experience, a medium-to-large organization will nearly always need to have a full-time Moodle administrator or developer in order to manage this system.

However, the total cost of ownership is normally considerably cheaper than comparable, commercial VLEs.

The open source component of Moodle really makes it the best VLE currently on the market, as this means that you effectively own the software and can make changes to it as long as you redistribute these changes back to the community. This is aligned with the academic community insofar as it fits in with academic principles of knowledge sharing and peer review. It also means that there are thousands of talented developers working every day of every week to improve the software. It also means that there have been thousands of modules built to add almost every feature you could ever wish for in Moodle. The commercial products are unlikely to be able to provide such a huge database of add-on extensions to their products.

What will you be doing?

In this book, you will be learning how to create themes for Moodle. You will start by learning how to change pre-installed Moodle themes and download new themes from various resources on the Internet. You will then learn how to edit these themes by using a mixture of **Hyper Text Markup Language (HTML)** and **Cascading Style Sheets (CSS)**. In part two of this book, you will then move on to creating a Moodle theme from scratch—from the planning stages to creating the graphics needed for your stunning new theme. You will then learn how to "slice and dice" your graphic design and use it to create a completely new theme for your Moodle site.

What skills will you need?

For the benefit of you and this book, the following assumptions have been made with regards to the skills required to edit and create themes for Moodle.

You will need to be reasonably familiar with HTML and CSS and have some exposure to graphics manipulation software packages. By any means, you do not have to be an expert, as Moodle theming is quite simple as long as you follow the instructions carefully. So if you have built websites before by using HTML and CSS, then you should hit the ground running. If you have only dabbled in web design before, you still shouldn't have any problems with the exercises in this book. If you are a total beginner, you can still do this. All you need to know is that you will need to take your time and make sure that you understand everything that you are learning before moving on through the book.

Tools for the job

None of the software packages suggested in this book are totally necessary and all can be supplanted with something else. However, if you can acquire or already have these tools, you will find the exercises much easier to follow.

Hardware

This may sound rather obvious but you are going to need a working Moodle installation, either as part of your organization's setup or as a local Moodle install. I would recommend a local Moodle installation, as this avoids the risk of bringing down your organization's Moodle server, and creates a more relaxed environment for you to work in. If anything untoward happens, you can just reinstall Moodle and start again.

If you haven't had any experience in installing Moodle, don't be too worried, as it is comparatively easy to install. There are various installation packages available on `Moodle.org` for most of the popular operating system platforms. Just choose the one that suits your computer setup, and follow the instructions carefully. I would recommend that you use the standard weekly install package and set up MySQL separately, rather than using the Windows install package because doing so will give you a better understanding of the platform and the install process. And in some respects this way is better because if you have any problems at a later stage, they will be easier to diagnose.

In case you have any problems, then use the community forums on `Moodle.org` to seek advice. You will be surprised how timely this advice will come.

Software

I have tried to keep the list of software needed to undertake the exercises in this book to a minimum. In fact, all of the software except Adobe Photoshop is free and open source, so all you will need to know is how to download and install these packages.

Adobe Photoshop

As suggested above, this is the only paid software package used in this book. Adobe Photoshop can be quite expensive, so if you do not have it, then it's worth trying to find out if your organization already has a spare license for it, or whether they would be prepared to purchase one for you to complete this project. In most cases, your organization will be prepared to do this for you, as it's a small cost when compared to the yearly salary paid to have a Moodle administrator or developer.

If it's not possible to get Adobe Photoshop, then there are various cheaper or free alternatives that you might be able to use. But the exercises will be hard unless you already know how to use your chosen graphics software. For instance, there is a cut-down version of Adobe Photoshop called "Adobe Elements", which is considerably cheaper. You could also have a look at "Paint Shop Pro" or the free "Gimp" image manipulation software. Just search on the Internet for these terms and you should be able to find the software relatively easy.

Firefox

My favorite web browser software is Mozilla Firefox. It is neat, free, and can be customized to suit everyone's web surfing needs. It is a great browser for budding or experienced web designers, and can be downloaded and installed in minutes. Mozilla Firefox has thousands of extensions, all of which are free and will increase your productivity as a Moodle themer by a magnitude of 10. In fact, there are tools such as Firebug that as a Moodle themer I simply could not do without.

FileZilla

If you are working directly on your organization's main Moodle server (which I do not really recommend), then you will need a **File Transfer Protocol** (FTP) software package so that you can move files, once edited, to the Moodle server. FileZilla again can be found by searching the Internet and what's more, it's free and can be downloaded and installed simply and quickly. If you use this method, then you will need to find out the login details for your Moodle server's FTP root folder. The server administrator will be able to give you this information.

Other web browsers

For testing purposes, you will need to have several other web browsers other than Windows Internet Explorer. I will spend a little more time on this a little later, and include details on where you can get these additional browsers. Suffice it to say that for now Google Chrome, Safari, and Opera are the other web browsers that you will need.

Summary

In summary, in this first chapter you have covered most of what there needs to be known about VLEs and Moodle. You have obviously already chosen Moodle, as you would not have bought this book otherwise. However, the preceding sections should help you to understand a little more about the Moodle application. You have learned about VLEs and their relationship to education: they are a tool used by educators to facilitate learning over the Internet. You have also learned about the different types of VLE that are available, and made some comparisons among these systems. You should now also understand what Moodle is and what advantages it has for teachers and learners.

Specifically, we covered:

- What VLEs are and what features we should expect from them
- We have looked into the different types of VLEs and the advantages that they offer over the traditional teaching and learning methods
- We have learned about Moodle and why we can use it
- Finally, we have learned what we will be doing in this book, what skills will be needed, and what tools will be required to work our way through the exercises.

Now that we've introduced Virtual Learning Environments and learned what Moodle can do for our organization, we can finally start to get our hands dirty and move on to some more interesting stuff, such as choosing and changing our first Moodle theme.

2
Moodle Themes

In this chapter, we will cover the basics of Moodle theming, including theme types, priority, location of the theme directory, and the concept of parent themes. We will also cover browsing and changing a theme within Moodle, and searching for, downloading, and installing custom themes. We will then finish off by changing the theme settings in the Moodle theme settings page. This is necessary because you will need a good understanding of how Moodle themes work to continue with the rest of the book and to be able to ultimately create your own theme(s) from scratch.

Here we shall cover:

◆ What is a Moodle theme?
◆ Browsing and selecting a Moodle theme
◆ Searching for and downloading a Moodle theme
◆ Installing a Moodle theme
◆ Changing Moodle's theme settings

So, let's get on with it...

Important preliminary points

For this chapter, it is expected that you will have access to a Moodle server, either local (on your own computer) or the live Moodle server that your organization is currently using. I recommend that you use a local copy of Moodle, so when you make changes, you do not compromise with the live server's availability. If you followed the advice that was given in the previous chapter, you have already set up your local Moodle site and are now ready to jump in.

What is a Moodle theme?

A **Moodle theme** is a template that controls the way Moodle looks. A theme can be changed by the Moodle administrator and can have its settings altered through the Moodle administrative interface. A theme does not normally affect the way Moodle functions, only the way it looks. You may have come across the term "theme" before in web applications such as **Content Management Systems** (**CMS**) and blogs such as WordPress, all of which have the ability to have their look or design changed through theming. WordPress, for example, has hundreds of themes available and many more that can be downloaded from various sites on the Internet. Examples of places from which you can search and download Moodle's themes on the Internet will be covered later in this chapter.

Theming as a concept for any web application is sometimes referred to as **skinning**. In general, these terms are used interchangeably and both refer to the separation of design (look and feel) from the functionality of the application. This way, changes to the theme or skin will have no effect on the application's ability to function as it is supposed to.

Some Moodle themers would argue that skinning is a slightly different way of controlling the look and feel of an application than theming insofar, as skinning is normally more separated from the application. Themes can be described as being a collection of files or a folder containing **HTML** (**Hyper Text Markup Language**) and **CSS** (**Cascading Style Sheets**) files, images, and other files such as scripts and skins. So, the theme would control the overall look and feel of an application and the skins would control the look and feel of the individual elements such as containers or blocks or even forums, wikis, or blogs. This system leverages the ultimate control over how an application looks, but unfortunately, Moodle doesn't readily employ this system at the time of writing (Moodle 1.9.4). It is believed that Moodle 2.0, when released, will employ something similar to skinning and will therefore leverage much more control over how Moodle can be customized.

Moodle comes with a set of free standard themes, though not all are as visually appealing as others. `Moodle.org` also has a large library of free downloadable themes, and there are many other third-party Moodle theme providers. Not all of these are free, but if they are not, they usually represent very good value for money. More on this later; for now, let's get going!

Browsing and selecting a Moodle theme

In this section, we will be browsing to our Moodle site, logging in as the administrative user, and navigating to the theme selector page. We will then go through the stages needed to choose a theme.

Time for action – browsing and selecting a Moodle theme

Okay, it's now time for some action. Open your local Moodle site and get familiar with Moodle's theming processes. I recommend that you use a locally installed Moodle to perform the exercises in the book, as you really do not want to risk crashing your organization's Moodle website.

1. Open your favorite browser and navigate to your local Moodle installation. If you followed the instructions on `Moodle.org`, then it will be at the following address: `http://localhost`. You should then be presented with your newly installed Moodle site, which should have loaded the default standard theme automatically, as seen in the following screenshot:

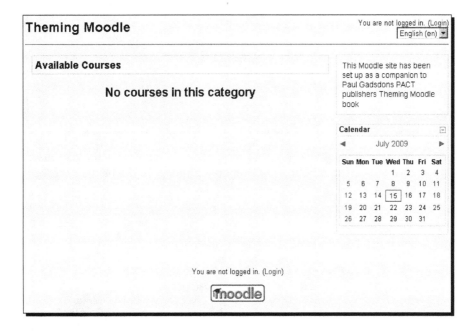

2. If you look at the top right-hand corner of your Moodle site, you will see this text: **You are not logged in. (Login).** If you click on the **Login** link (in blue), it will take you to the login screen, as seen below:

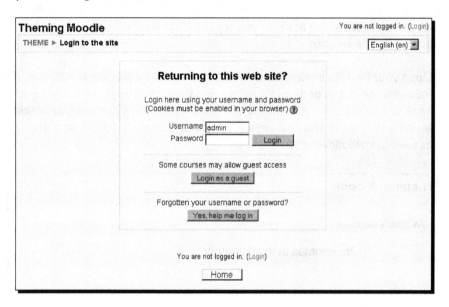

3. Enter your administrative username and password in the relevant text boxes. Then click on the **Login** button and something similar to the next screenshot will be displayed:

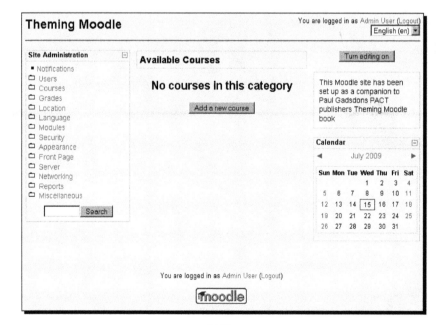

4. To choose and change a Moodle theme, you should go to the administration block and choose: **Appearance | Themes | Theme Selector**, as seen on the left-hand side of the image below:

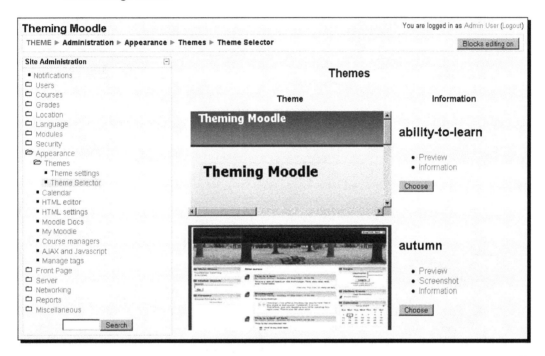

5. You should now see a list of all the themes that are installed. You may also notice an image of each theme to help you get an idea of what the theme looks like. Take a minute to scroll down the page and look at the installed themes and identify one that you like. It might also be a good idea to write some notes on what exactly you liked about the theme. Doing this will help you identify design ideas for your own theme. Choose a theme, and you will see how easy it is to change a theme for your Moodle site. One of my favorite Moodle themes is called "Custom Corners." Go ahead and choose **Custom Corners** by scrolling down the page until you can see the "Custom Corners" theme. Choose the "Custom Corners" theme by clicking on the **Choose** button on the right-hand side of the "Custom Corners" theme image. You should now see information about the new theme load.

6. Click on the **Continue** button to get a look at your new Moodle theme, as seen below:

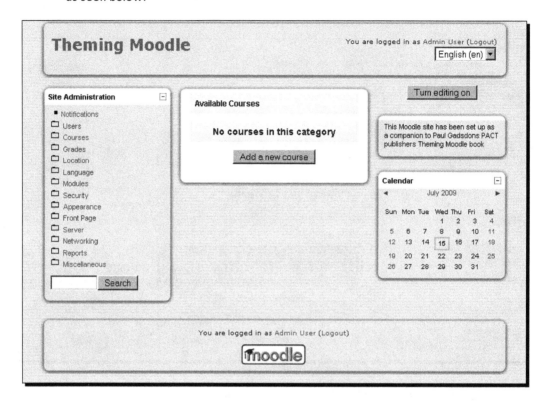

What just happened?

What have you just learned? Well, you have just learned to open up the Moodle Course Management System in your favorite web browser and navigate to your local (not live on the Web) Moodle site. You have also learned how to log in and use the administration block to make changes to Moodle's configuration. Finally, you have browsed to the theme selector and learned to change the current default Moodle theme to another one.

Have a go hero – choosing a few other themes

Try to browse to the theme chooser on your Moodle site and choose a different site theme. Continue choosing different themes until you become comfortable with the process.

Theme types

Themes are similar to Moodle's roles insofar as they are assigned to different contexts such as site, user, course, and category, and can often be set at any of these levels. So, Moodle can be customized to have a different course or category theme than its site theme.

Site themes	Site themes are site-wide themes that only the Moodle administrator can choose. They are available at **Administration | Themes | Theme Selector**.
User themes	User themes can be set via the **Theme settings** page. If the **allowuserthemes** capability is enabled, a user or student can choose his/her own theme, which will be used instead of the site theme (unless a specific course theme is set by the instructor). The **allowuserthemes** capability is set by clicking on the **Allow user themes** checkbox at **Site Administration | Themes | Theme settings**. When enabled, users may choose their user theme by viewing their user profile page, moving to **Edit profile**, clicking on the **Advanced** button, selecting a theme from the **Preferred theme** drop-down list, and finally, clicking on the **Update profile** button.
Course themes	Again, course themes can be set via the **Theme settings** page. If the **allowcoursethemes** is set, then the editing teacher can change the course theme to the one they prefer. This will then force all of the users of the course to see this theme rather than the one set through 'site themes' or 'user themes'. This is done by checking the **Allow course themes** checkbox in the **Theme settings** page at **Site Administration | Themes | Theme settings**.
Category themes	Category theme setting was introduced in Moodle 1.9. It gives the administrator the ability to set a theme for an entire category of courses. For example, each department within a university could create and set its own themes that filter through all of the courses in that department or category. Category themes are disabled by default because they require additional processing (database-related overhead).

Session themes	Session themes are perhaps the most powerful and arguably the most useful of the Moodle theme types. These themes can be set by session data, which essentially means that the theme is loaded only on each individual visit by a user. The session theme is set by appending a string of text to the end of the URL and can therefore identify different themes for different users or situations. For instance, if someone is using a mobile phone to access a course within Moodle, the latter can automatically load a specific custom-built theme created for mobile devices. No user or administrative intervention would be required. For example, you can offer a link for iPhone users who utilize the session theme. Moodle will then automatically load the theme that is set in the URL (if one is provided). In a standard Moodle installation, session themes are not active. To activate them, the administrator must add the parameter `$CFG->allowthemechangeonurl = true;` to the Moodle `config.php` file in the Moodle root directory.
Page themes	Page themes are set only by code and are therefore not implemented often in Moodle installations. They are themes that are set for specific pages with Moodle. `Moodle.org` suggests that these themes have been added only for completeness.

Theme priority

Theme priority is the order in which Moodle loads and applies the different themes. Theme priority is a relatively new concept, introduced in Moodle 1.9. The `config.php` file is used to control the priority of themes and by default, it is set through the following code in the `config.php` file:

```
$CFG->themeorder = array('page', 'course', 'category', 'session',
                         'user', 'site');
```

For instance, if you build a Moodle site for a specific device such as a PDA, you might want the 'session' theme to load first.

Parent themes

Parent themes in Moodle utilize the powerful mechanism of CSS to reuse parts of a Moodle theme and create a new derivative called a **child theme**. Parent and child themes can be used to create variations of a theme that support different styles needed for differing visual impairments and color blindness.

In order to use parent themes, the site administrator will have to modify the `$THEME->parent` and `$THEME->parentsheets` variables in the theme's `config.php` file.

Theme directory

The Moodle theme directory can be found at: `C:\Program Files\Apache Software Foundation\Apache2.2\htdocs\theme\`.

This directory has the following core themes as standard:

- cornflower
- chameleon
- custom_corners
- formal_white
- metal
- oceanblue
- orangewhite
- orangewhitepda
- standard
- standardblue
- standardgreen
- standardlogo
- standardred
- standardwhite
- wood

What is in a standard Moodle theme folder? They are often different, but they normally contain at least some common files and folders.

Time for action – browsing the 'Standard' theme folder

The next exercise has been designed to make you familiar with the structure of the main Moodle directory and to make sure that you know where the theme's directory is. It is a very simple stage in this book, but it is required because depending on where and how your original Moodle has been set up, the main Moodle directory may not be in the same place.

1. Go to your desktop and double-click on the **My Computer** icon. If you are using Windows Vista, click on the **Start** button and then click **Computer**. This will open up the 'My Computer' dialog box.

2. Now browse to `C:\Program Files\Apache Software Foundation\Apache2.2\htdocs`. This will open the main Moodle site's directory.

3. Now click on the `theme` directory. It will open and list all of the themes that come packaged with Moodle.

4. Finally, click on the `standard` theme folder. You should see the same file structure as seen in the following screenshot:

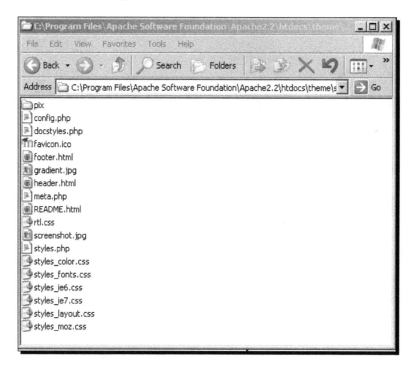

What just happened?

Hopefully, you have learned about the different Moodle theme types, what theme types mean, and how you can use them to allow the user to customize their Moodle experience. We have discussed the concepts of *theme priority* and *parent themes*. Finally, you learned how to browse to the `theme` folder in the main Moodle directory and had a look at the different themes installed by default in Moodle.

Here is a description of the content of the `standard` theme folder that you have just opened.

The pix folder

The `pix` folder typically contains the images used in a Moodle theme. These include images or pictures and any icons that are used in the theme.

config.php

This file contains the configuration settings for your Moodle theme. The `config.php` file inside your Moodle `theme` directory is not to be confused with the main Moodle's `config.php` file that resides in the root directory of the server.

meta.php

The `meta.php` file detects whether the user is using Internet Explorer 6 or 7 and loads either `styles_ie6.css` or `styles_ie7.css`, respectively. This is done due to the differences in the way different web browsers interpret CSS Web standards. We will cover more on CSS later in this book.

doctyles.php

This file is now redundant, as it was used in much earlier versions of Moodle and has been kept for backward compatibility. So, depending on the Moodle theme that you choose, it may or may not be present.

screenshot.jpg

This file is an image of the completed skin so that the Moodle site administrator can see what the theme looks like before he or she chooses it.

favicon.ico

This is the small icon that is shown before the site's URL in the browser's address bar.

README.html

This is an HTML file that typically provides an overview of the theme's features and/ or installation instructions. The `README.html` file is displayed when you click on the **Information** link while selecting a theme.

header/footer.html

These two files are the editable files, therefore you can change the top and bottom of your Moodle site to suit your own needs. Among other things, they contain elements such as the logo, header text, login text, jump menu, and the navigation bar. These files will likely be the first files that you will change when creating or changing a theme for Moodle. See the following screenshots depicting the header and footer areas in the standard Moodle theme:

Header area:

Footer area:

styles_moz.css

This is a standard CSS file that controls the presentation of Mozilla Firefox-specific styles. It is normally used because different web browsers interpret CSS rules in different ways. Therefore, sometimes it is necessary to write slightly different CSS for Mozilla Firefox.

styles_ie6.css

This is a standard CSS file that controls the presentation of Windows Internet Explorer 6-specific styles.

styles_ie7.css

This is a standard CSS file that controls the presentation of Windows Internet Explorer 7-specific styles.

styles_fonts.css

The `styles_fonts.css` file is a stylesheet that defines the font style rules used throughout a Moodle theme.

styles_color.css

The `styles_color.css` file is a stylesheet that defines the style rules for the colors used throughout a Moodle theme.

styles_layout.css

The `styles_layout.css` file is a stylesheet that defines the layout style rules used throughout a Moodle theme.

rtl.css

The `rtl.css` file is an interesting one. It contains the layout definitions required for right-to-left languages (for example, Hebrew). It overrides definitions in other files to move right-floating blocks to the left, align text to the right, swap left and right margins, and so on.

Searching for and downloading Moodle themes

Searching for and downloading Moodle themes is a great way of making your Moodle site look different than the standard pre-installed themes. There are literally thousands of Moodle themes available on the Internet, if you know where to look.

As with pre-installed Moodle themes, many of the themes that you can download from the Internet are free, and all of them are also open source. This means that you can usually download them freely and change them to suit your needs. However, it is worth noting that open source doesn't usually mean that there aren't any restrictions or copyrights placed on the work. Most open source software or code available on the Internet is copyrighted and does normally have some sort of restriction on use. You may be required to leave the copyright credits in the code (attribution) to use only what you have downloaded for non-commercial purposes. **Attribution** is the concept of requiring the author to be credited, so, in this context, it is important that you take the time to look at the terms and conditions of any software or code that you download from the Internet. These are normally placed in a `README.html` or `license.txt` file in the downloaded folder or at the top of the code, if only a single file.

Although most of the Moodle themes on the Internet are free (not all of them are) and there is a growing community of theming companies or individuals that create commercial themes for the Moodle industry, these themes would still be open source, that is, you would just be paying for the time spent on the development of these themes. We will cover the purchasing of Moodle themes in the next section. For now, concentrate on searching and finding a wider variety of themes that come installed with a default Moodle installation.

Time for action – searching for Moodle themes

In this exercise, you are going to visit the primary resource on the Internet for Moodle themes. If you still have your web browser open, I recommend opening either a new browser window or a new tab.

In your browser, navigate to the Moodle website `http://www.moodle.org`. Go to the top menu and hover your mouse over the **Downloads** link. On the right-hand side, you will see that the menu drops down and displays further pages that are available. Choose the **Themes** section, which is second from the bottom. This will take you to the **Themes** page of the Moodle database, where you will be able to download the themes shared by other members of the Moodle community. You can see this exemplified in the following screenshot:

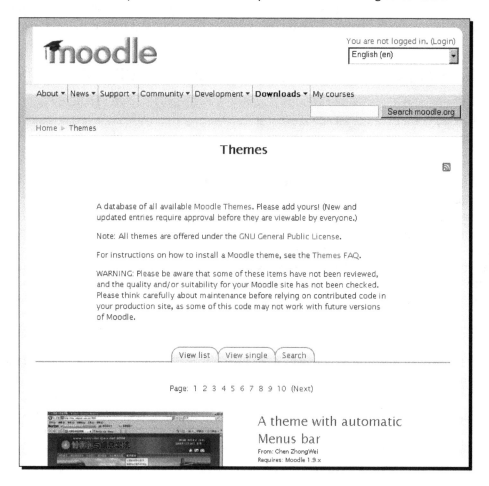

What just happened?

In this exercise, you have learned how to browse to the main Moodle.org website and navigate to the Moodle themes database. You can see that there are a lot of themes freely available to download and use. You are encouraged to review the terms and conditions of any of the themes that you intend to download and use.

As you can see, there are over 100 Moodle themes listed here. I personally like the *Anomaly* theme by *New School Learning* or the *Autumn* and *Lipp* themes by *Patrick Malley*. Have a good look through these themes, as this will help you to get a good idea of what can be achieved through Moodle theming.

Installing a new Moodle theme

In this section, you will continue from where we left off by choosing a theme from the Moodle themes database. You will then download the *Autumn* theme, extract the downloaded ZIP file, and then install the theme on your Moodle installation. Finally, you will go to the theme selector and choose your newly downloaded theme to change the look of your Moodle site.

I suspect that after previewing some of the themes, you have a few favorite themes from the large selection offered on Moodle.org. Now, I want you to choose a theme that you like from this theme database. If you have navigated away from the Moodle theme database, go to http://moodle.org/mod/data/view.php?d=26.

Time for action – downloading a new Moodle theme

Now, for the benefit of this book, I have decided to choose the *Autumn* theme by *Patrick Malley* because it's a professional looking theme. You may download any other theme; please go ahead and do so. The process that you will be going through to do this should be similar for any of the chosen theme.

1. Scroll through the list of themes until you have reached the *Autumn* theme by *Patrick Malley*.

2. Click on the sample theme image or the link entitled **autumn** to the right of the image.

3. Now click on the **Download** link.

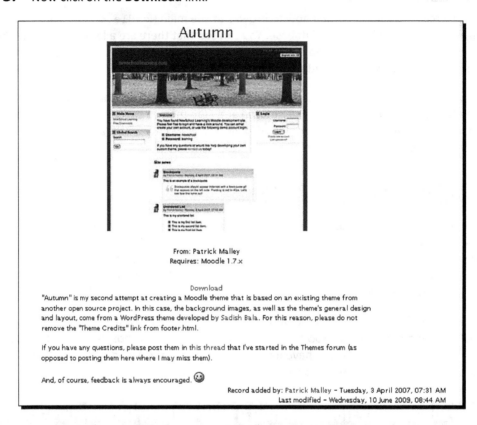

4. Depending on your browser (Mozilla Firefox, Windows Internet Explorer, and so on), you will normally see a download dialog box asking if you want to open or save the file, as seen in the following screenshot:

Mozilla Firefox:

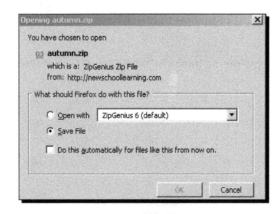

Windows Internet Explorer:

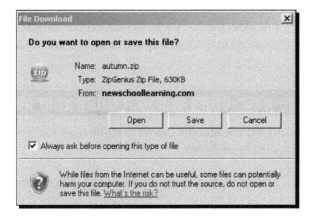

5. Click on the **Save** button, seen above, to download the theme's ZIP file to your `Downloads` directory (make sure to note the path where you are saving the file).

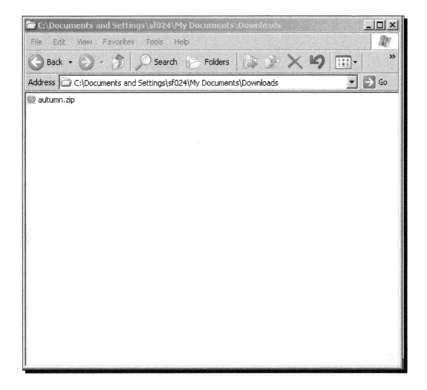

What just happened?

You have just visited the Moodle theme database and downloaded a ZIP file containing the *Autumn* theme by *Patrick Malley*. The ZIP file was saved in your `Downloads` directory. In Windows, this is typically located in the `My Documents` folder. You are now ready for the next exercise.

Time for action – extracting and installing your Moodle theme

In this section, you will extract the Moodle theme that you have just downloaded, and you will install it in your Moodle `theme` folder.

1. Navigate to the folder to which you have downloaded the Moodle theme and extract it by using your computer's ZIP extraction software. You may have WinZip or you may be using Windows' own ZIP software. If you have left the download location as the default location, then your *Autumn* theme ZIP file will be in the `Downloads` directory of the `My Documents` folder, as seen below:

2. Right-click on the `autumn.zip` file, roll your mouse over **ZipGenius**, and a context menu will appear. Choose **Extract Here.**

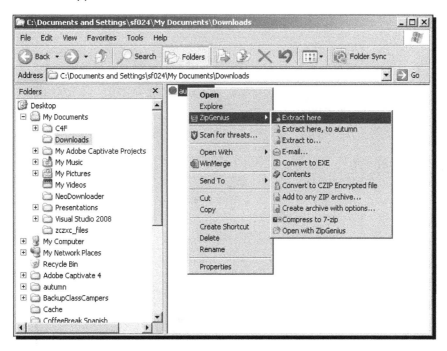

3. Right-click on the `autumn` folder and choose **Copy**.

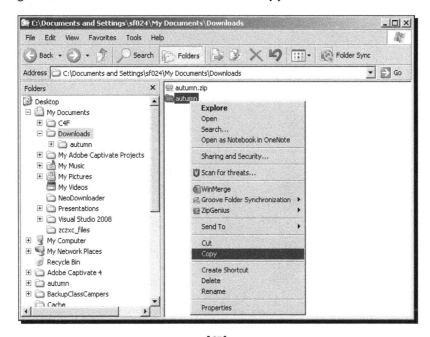

4. Now, navigate to the `theme` folder inside your Moodle installation folder. If you followed the installation instructions on Moodle, this should be in `C:\Program Files\Apache Software Foundation\Apache\htdocs\theme`. Once you are in the `theme` folder, you can right-click again and choose **Paste**. This should copy your *Autumn* theme in your `theme` folder within your Moodle installation, as seen below:

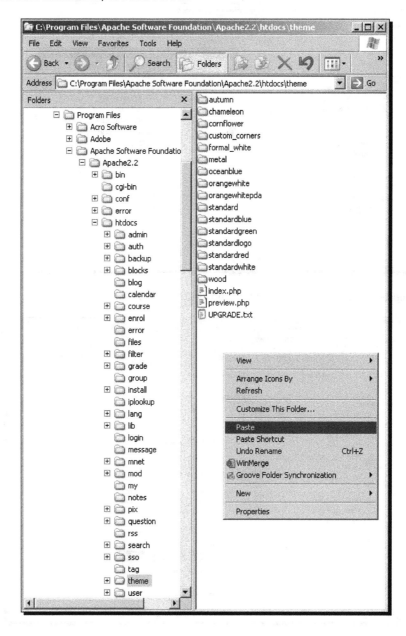

5. Open your favorite web browser and navigate to `http://localhost`. Now, your Moodle site should load into the browser.

6. Log in again as a site administrator—the login that you used when setting up Moodle or the one given to you by the Moodle server administrator.

7. As mentioned earlier, go to the administration block on the left-hand side and choose **Appearance | Themes | Theme Selector**. You will now see the **Theme Selector** page. The themes are ordered alphabetically, so the *Autumn* theme should be near the top.

8. Finally, click on the **Choose** button to the right of the theme image. Your new theme should look like the following screenshot:

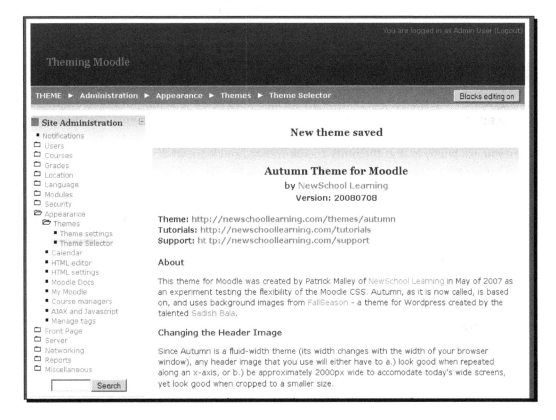

What just happened?

In this exercise, you have navigated to the `autumn.zip` file and extracted the files. You then copied the extracted files to your site's Moodle `theme` directory, thus installing it. You then opened up your local Moodle installation in your web browser and chose your new theme to be the current theme.

Have a go hero – download and install another theme

Go back to the Moodle.org website and download a couple of new themes that interest you or catch your eye. Once you have downloaded the themes (refer back to the instructions described previously in this chapter, if needed), install the new themes on your Moodle site. One by one, select the newly installed Moodle themes and navigate around your site to see how they look.

Have a go hero – find and install some other themes

Finally, with your preferred search engine (for example, Google or MSN) try searching for free Moodle themes. You might be surprised to see how many are there on the Internet. Once you have found one, review the terms and limitations, and if you agree, download the theme and install it.

Moodle's theme settings

In this chapter, the last subject that we are going to look at is the administration of Moodle's theme settings. First, you will change one of the main theme settings, namely the **Theme list** setting, so you can see how this change affects the working of the Moodle theming system. Then you will briefly look at the other theme settings and learn what each setting will do. The **Theme settings** page can be found by navigating to: **Site Administration | Appearance | Themes | Theme settings.**

Time for action – forcing users to use your theme choices

Now, you are going to change the **Theme list** setting and test to see how the change actually works. This setting will restrict the amount of themes available to any given user. For instance, you may want the teacher role to be able to change themes in a course, but only want a restricted amount of themes to be used. Restricting the number of available themes is useful because some of the themes may not be consistent with the site.

1. Navigate to the **Theme settings** page at: **Appearance | Themes | Theme settings**. The following screenshot displays the **Theme settings** page.

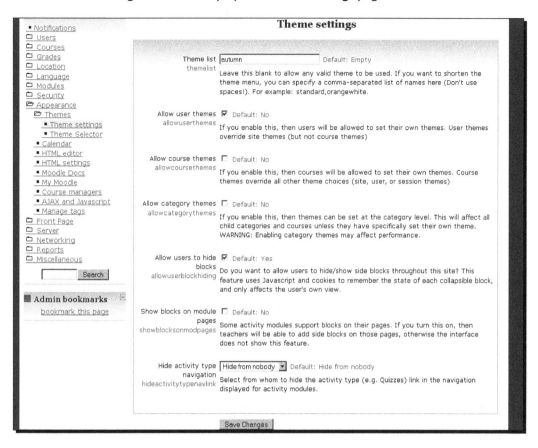

2. Now, add the name of the theme that you are using currently in the **Theme list** text box at the top of the **Theme settings** page, as seen below. This is case-sensitive if you are using a Linux server.

3. Press the **Save Changes** button at the bottom of the page and you should see the confirmation message appear on the page on which you currently are.

4. Now, in order to test this, you will need to log in as a test student or teacher. As the default user is student, it will be easier at this stage to add a new student user. Navigate to **Site Administration | Users | Accounts | Add a new user** and you should see the following page. The fields marked in red are the required fields and will have to be filled in.

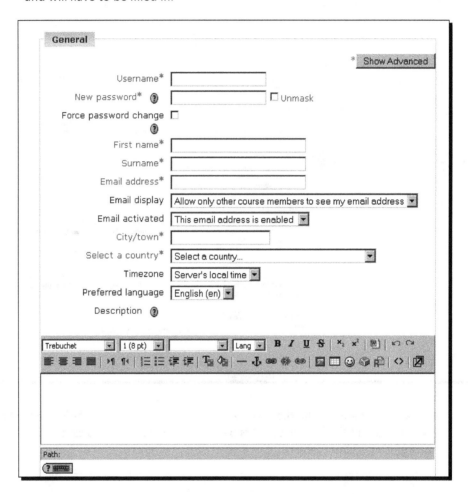

5. Fill in the required fields with the following information. There is no need to fill in the other fields.

Username: johndoe

New password: johndoe

First name: john

Surname: doe

Email address: johndoe@ johndoe.com

City/town: anything

Select a Country: Any country

6. Click on the **Update profile** button at the bottom of the page. You have now added a new Moodle student user, so you can test the theme list settings that you have just changed.

7. The next step is to browse to John Doe's user profile and log in as that user. Immediately after you add John Doe as a student user, you will be directed to the accounts page that lists the current Moodle users. To log in as any user on this page, just click on the user you want—in this case, it will be John Doe and you will be directed to that user's profile page, which will look like the following screenshot:

8. Now, just click on the **Login as** button at the bottom of the screen, and you will be logged in as that user.

9. Click on the **john doe** link at the top-right corner of the page, as seen below:

10. Click on the **Edit profile** tab at the top of the page.

11. Click on the **Show Advanced** button on the right-hand side. You will now see the profile page again, but with a little more information, including the **Preferred theme** drop-down box right at the bottom of the first section.

12. Click on the **Preferred theme** drop-down box and you should see that there are now only two themes to choose from, namely **Default** and **autumn**, as seen below:

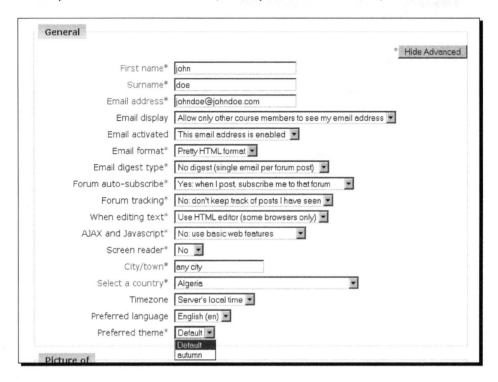

What just happened?

In this section, you have changed the **Theme list** setting to restrict the number of themes available to the users through either user or course theme.

You subsequently added a new student user to Moodle and logged in as that user. You had to do this because you needed to check whether the change in your theme list setting had been applied. You went to the new student's profile and checked to see if the change had been reflected in the **Preferred theme** drop-down box.

Thus, you successfully restricted the amount of themes that are available to the student or teacher within Moodle.

Theme settings list

There are several other theme settings listed on the theme settings page, so have a look at what each of these do. Additional information on Moodle's theme settings can be found at `http://docs.moodle.org/en/Theme_settings`.

Theme list

As demonstrated, the **Theme list** text box is used to control how many and exactly which themes appear in the theme lists for course and user themes. The user themes are the selectable themes in the **User profile** section when a user edits his or her profile. The course themes are available to administrators and teachers within the course settings page. Both of these themes can be set independently from the main Moodle site theme if allowed by the administrator.

If this text box is left empty, all of the default themes will be available. But, if you wish, you can restrict which themes appear by specifying a comma-separated list of the themes, such as autumn, standard, and orangewhite.

Allow user themes

The **Allow user themes** checkbox, if set, will allow a Moodle user to choose their own themes from their profile page. User themes will override site themes, but not course themes.

Allow course themes

If you enable this, teachers will be able to set their own themes for the courses they teach. If they do, then it will make no difference what theme a user chooses in their profile, as this will override their theme selection. Therefore, course themes override all other theme selections including site, user, or session themes.

Allow category themes

If enabled, this setting will set a theme at a category level and will override the course theme setting unless it has been specifically set by the teacher. This setting can be used so that departments can have their own look and feel within Moodle. You have probably noticed a warning next to this setting insofar as it suggests that this setting may affect Moodle's performance. So, I would suggest that you use this with caution, especially on sites with a large number of courses and/or course categories and subcategories.

Allow users to hide blocks

This setting allows the user to show and hide blocks throughout the site, and it uses a mixture of JavaScript and cookies to remember these user settings. So, use this with caution. Users need to have JavaScript and cookies enabled in their web browsers for this setting to work. Another issue with this setting is that users are likely to forget that they have hidden a block and ask for technical support because they can't find them.

Show blocks on module pages

Some activity modules support blocks on their pages. If you turn this on, teachers will be able to add sideblocks on those pages; otherwise, the interface does not show this feature.

Hide activity type navigation

Select from whom to hide the activity type (for example, quizzes) link in the navigation displayed for activity modules. This setting is used to hide activity type navigation links in the breadcrumb, as they are not overly useful to an ordinary user.

Pop quiz

Q1. In the **Site administration** block, how does one navigate to the *Theme selector*?

    A. **Front Page | Front Page settings**

    B. **Server | Environment**

    C. **Appearance | My Moodle**

    D. **Appearance | Themes | Theme Selector**

Q2. There is another way of restricting the users from picking any themes from within their profile. How would this be done?

    A. Remove all of the unwanted themes from the **Theme list** in the **Theme settings** page

    B. Delete all but the theme being used from the Moodle theme folder

    C. Remove the **Preferred theme** from the profile page

Q3. Why do you have to use *category themes* with caution?

    A. Because it would ruin the overall look and feel of Moodle

    B. Category administrators could change the theme for Moodle's home page

    C. Because it takes a lot of server overhead to traverse through all the different categories and subcategories.

Have a go hero – you are on your own

Now that you have finished this chapter, you should know how to choose a theme within Moodle. You can search for, download, and extract the files to your Moodle site's theme directory. Essentially, you now know how to search for, download, and install new themes for your site. Have a go at the following challenges and see if you can put into practice what you have learned.

Summary

In short, we have covered how to switch, download, and install Moodle's themes. You should now be fairly confident that if asked, you could choose a different site theme for Moodle, find new themes on the Internet, and install those themes on your Moodle site.

Specifically, we covered:

◆ What a Moodle theme is and what its relationship is with the main Moodle application.

◆ You have learned how easy it is to log in to Moodle as the administrator and to navigate to the Moodle themes' selector page and choose a Moodle theme.

◆ You should now know the difference between *site*, *user, course, category, session*, and *page* themes and how they can be prioritized. You have also learned about parent themes and briefly looked at where the theme directory is and what is in it.

◆ You then learned to search for a Moodle theme and downloaded it. After this, you learned how to extract and install your new theme in Moodle.

◆ Finally, you looked at the theme settings page and undertook some exercises to learn how to restrict the number of themes that are available to the site users.

Now that you've learned about Moodle themes, we will move on to Chapter 3, where you will learn how to change the header and footer XHTML files for a particular theme. You are going to create your own theme using one of the standard themes as a base.

3
Customizing the Header and Footer

This chapter will cover the steps needed to make changes to the `header.html` *and* `footer.html` *files in the* `theme` *directory of your Moodle site. You will start by making some small changes, such as changing the logo and the title text so that you can see how easy it is to customize the header in Moodle. You will also look at some basic HTML recommendations to keep your Moodle theme standards-compliant. After this, you will move on to changing the footer, including removing the Moodle logo and the login information links and adding your own copyright or footer text. Finally, in this chapter, you will learn to check that your changes are standards-compliant and look similar in more than one web browser.*

In this chapter, you shall:

- ◆ Replace the Moodle logo with your own
- ◆ Replace the title text with your own
- ◆ Replace the footer logo and remove the login link
- ◆ Add your own customized footer information
- ◆ Download a different web browser
- ◆ Test your changes in several web browsers

So, let's get on with it...

Important preliminary points

In order to continue with the exercises in the chapter, you will need to understand the importance of web browser compatibility. All web browsers are different, and most of them handle HTML and Cascading Style Sheets (CSS) differently. It is not so much that one web browser is better than another or that one web browser is more accurate at rendering HTML or CSS. Rather, it's that CSS rules are often interpreted differently by software developers who designed these browsers. For web developers and designers, this can be very annoying, but an unfortunate and inevitable reality.

So, to make sure that the changes that you make to Moodle's theme files are the same or similar across most of the major web browsers, you will need to install various web browsers, such as Firefox, Internet Explorer, Chrome, Opera, Safari, and so on, and make sure that you remember to test your changes. You shall learn to install the required web browsers as you work through this chapter.

Customizing the header

One of the first tasks that you will be asked to do concerning Moodle theming is to customize the main Moodle header file. Most people start by learning to change the Moodle logo for one of their own. The file that you will be editing in the first part of this chapter is the `header.html` file. For this chapter, you will assume the *standard theme* that comes with Moodle.

Time for action – making a copy of the standard theme

In this exercise, you will be making a copy of the standard theme so that you can make changes to it without interfering with Moodle's theming process. You need to do this because many of the Moodle themes use the standard theme as the base theme.

1. Navigate to the folder: `C:\Program Files\Apache Software Foundation\ Apache 2.2\htdocs\theme`.

2. Right-click on the `standard` theme folder and choose **Copy**, as seen in the following screenshot:

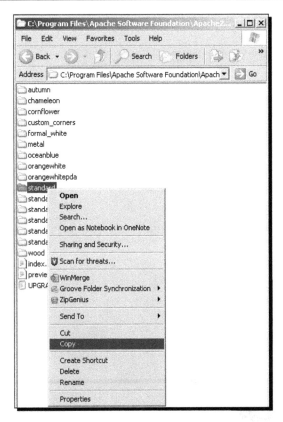

3. Right-click again in some empty space and choose **Paste**. The copied `standard` theme will be replicated and have the name `Copy of standard`, as seen below:

4. Right-click on this folder and choose **Rename** to rename the folder to `mytheme`.

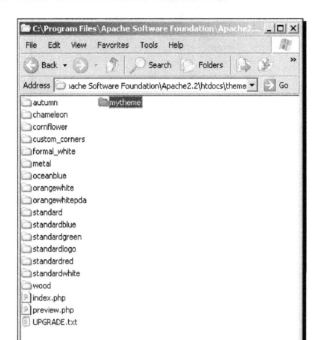

What just happened?

You have just made a copy of the *standard* theme that comes with Moodle and have relocated and renamed the theme, so you can now make some basic changes without interfering with any other themes in the `theme` directory. Most themes use the standard theme as the parent theme and then build upon this styled theme. So, if you were to change this theme directly, you would probably mess up most of the themes that are installed in your Moodle site.

Adding your own logo

Now that you have made a copy of the standard theme, you will go on and replace the Moodle logo with your own. Most often, your organization will have a logo that you can use; perhaps you could just copy one from their website. An important point to note here is that the logo that you use should be in the GIF or `.png` format.

The following figure has been created with Adobe Photoshop to demonstrate that it would be best to create a very basic logo if you don't have one.

Time for action – copying your logo to your mytheme directory

1. Navigate to the location of your logo.

2. Right-click and choose **Copy**.

3. Navigate to your Moodle site's \theme\mytheme\pix directory, right-click, and choose **Paste**. The result should resemble the following screenshot:

What just happened?

In this very simple exercise, you have copied the logo that you had or created and placed it in the correct directory in your new mytheme directory. This is now ready for you to use in the header.html file to display your logo.

Now you will edit the main header.html file to include your new logo. The header.html file can be found in your site's \theme\mytheme directory.

Time for action – adding the logo code to your header.html file

1. Navigate to your `mytheme` directory, right-click on the `header.html` file, and choose **Open With | WordPad**.

2. Open the `header.html` file with your favorite text editor (WordPad, Notepad, Vim, and so on). As a Windows shortcut, you can right-click on the `header.html` file and choose **Open With | WordPad**, as seen below:

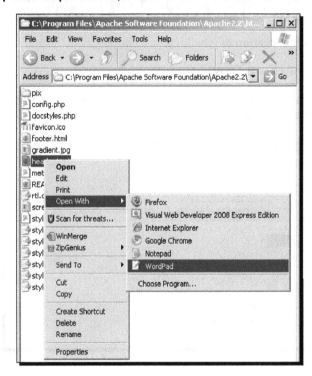

Top Tip – Text editors

We have chosen WordPad here as it retains the original markup format. Notepad, on the other hand, can be difficult to use, as it lacks some of the functionalities of WordPad. If you already use another text or HTML editor, then please use it. It's about familiarity here, so it's always best to use that with which you feel comfortable.

3. Find the following lines of code:

```php
<?php print_container_start(true, '', 'header-home'); ?>
    <h1 class="headermain"><?php echo $heading ?></h1>
    <div class="headermenu"><?php echo $menu ?></div>
<?php print_container_end(); ?>
```

4. Insert the following line of code:

```
<img src="<?php echo $CFG->themewww .'/'. current_theme() ?>/pix/
logo.gif" alt="Institutions Logo" />
```

Immediately after:

```
<h1 class="headermain">
```

As shown here:

```
<?php print_container_start(true, '', 'header-home'); ?>
  <h1 class="headermain">
    <img src="<?php echo $CFG->themewww .'/'.
      current_theme() ?>/pix/logo.gif" alt="Institutions Logo" />
    <?php echo $heading ?></h1>
  <div class="headermenu"><?php echo $menu ?></div>
<?php print_container_end(); ?>
```

You can download this code from the Packt website.

5. Save and close `header.html`.

6. Open your web browser and type in the URL of your local Moodle site.

7. Change the current theme, which should be *Autumn*, to your theme by navigating to **Appearance | Themes | Theme Selector** and choosing `mytheme`. You should see something similar to the following screenshot, but with your own logo.

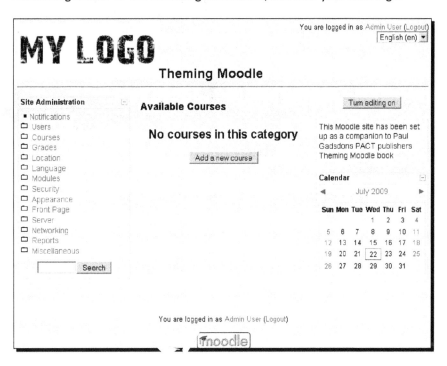

What just happened?

In this exercise, you have learned where a theme's `header.html` file is and how to open the `header.html` file for editing. You also learned what part of the code you should change in order to have your own logo appear on the front page of your Moodle site.

Have a go hero – adding another logo

Again, it's time for you to have a go at changing and modifying some of the things that you have learned through this chapter. First, it would be a good idea for you to try to create a new logo and add it to the `header.html` file in your `mytheme` folder. This time, leave the inner page header as it is.

Top Tip – Two headers

During this exercise, you may have noticed that the `header.html` file has two instances of the following line of code: `<h1 class="headermain">`. This is because Moodle loads a slightly different header depending on whether you are on the front page or any other page within the site. This means that the changes you have made will only be visible on the front page and not on any other page. Go and check this by opening your local Moodle site and clicking on the **Logout** link in the top right-hand corner, and then clicking the **Login** link in the same place. This will take you to the login front page of Moodle, where you will notice that your logo isn't where it is supposed to be. In most situations, you would want to have your logo on all pages within your Moodle site, so you will have to replicate the last exercise and paste your logo code in the other instance of `<h1 class="headermain">`.

Time for action – adding the logo code to your header.html file again!

1. Navigate to your `mytheme` directory, right-click on the `header.html` file, and choose **Open With | WordPad**.

2. Open with a text editor (that is, WordPad or other), as seen below:

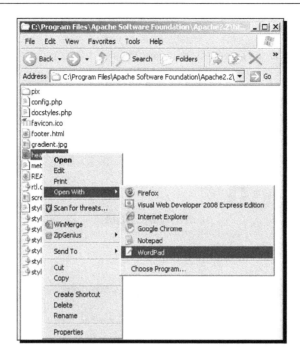

3. Find the following lines of code:

```php
<?php print_container_start(true, '', 'header'); ?>
    <h1 class="headermain"><?php echo $heading ?></h1>
    <div class="headermenu"><?php echo $menu ?></div>
<?php print_container_end(); ?>
```

4. Insert the following line of code:

```php
<img src="<?php echo $CFG->themewww .'/'. current_theme() ?>/pix/
logo.gif" alt="Institutions Logo" />
```

Immediately after:

```php
<h1 class="headermain">
```

As shown:

```php
<?php print_container_start(true, '', 'header'); ?>
    <h1 class="headermain">
    <img src="<?php echo $CFG->themewww .'/'.
      current_theme() ?>/pix/logo.gif" alt="Institutions Logo" />
    <?php echo $heading ?></h1>
    <div class="headermenu"><?php echo $menu ?></div>
<?php print_container_end(); ?>
```

You can download this code from the Packt website.

5. Save and close `header.html`.

6. If you haven't already opened your Moodle site, then open your web browser and type in the URL of your local Moodle site.

7. Navigate to any other page in your site or click on the **Logout** and **Login** links on the top right-hand corner, and this time you should see the main login page with your logo, as shown in the following screenshot:

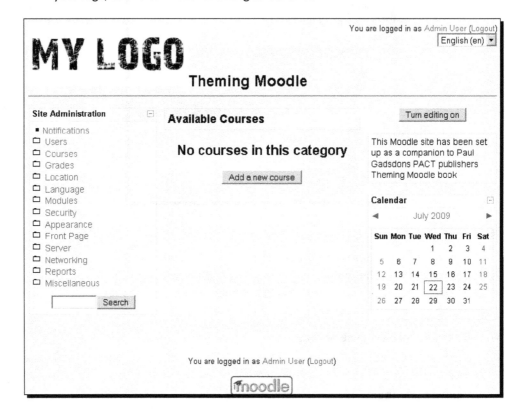

What just happened?

You added the logo code to the second instance of the theme's Moodle header. Both instances are in the same theme `header.html` file, and they load depending on whether the user is on the front page or any inner Moodle pages.

Have a go hero - putting back the inner page title

Now try to go back to your `header.html` file and comment out the inner page header code so that it does not load the inner page title. This will hopefully make you more familiar with editing the `header.html` file.

Making your own Moodle logo visible

Now, wherever you go within your Moodle site, your own logo should be visible on all Moodle pages.

The next thing you want to do is to change the title text in the `header.html` file within your `theme` directory. By default, the site's name text is generated automatically by Moodle and is dependent on the site name that was added when installing Moodle (front page), or the site name and course's short name (course pages). The front page title can be changed at any stage by navigating to: **Administration | Front Page | Front Page settings**.

However, Moodle themers may want to add their own title text to the front page, or to all inner pages, or even both. Having your own title text on the front page, for instance, is used when the Moodle's front page is being used as a general welcome page and doesn't have any Moodle courses loaded.

Top Tip – Commenting out code

In the following exercise, you will be changing the core code of the `header.html` file. It is worth pointing out that rather than deleting code from this file, it is best to comment out the parts of the code that you don't want to use. This way, you always have the original code to fall back on.

There are two different types of comments in Moodle theme files: HTML comments and PHP comments. In order to comment out a piece of code that is outside a section of PHP code—`<?php - code in here ?>`—you will need to wrap the code in HTML comments:

```
<!--<?php - code in here ?>-->
```

However, if the code you need to comment out is inside of a section of PHP code, for example:

```
<?php }
     echo $loggedinas; - line to comment
     echo $homelink;
<?php }
```

Then you should use:

```
<?php }
     /*echo $loggedinas;*/
     echo $homelink;
<?php }
```

This will render the code line obsolete—the web server can't see it, but it is still there for you to uncomment if you wish to use it again.

Time for action – changing the title text

1. Navigate to your `mytheme` directory, right-click on the `header.html` file, and choose **Open With | WordPad**, as seen below:

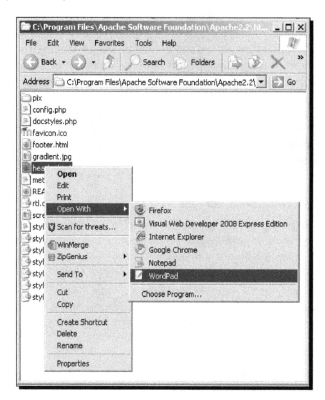

2. Find the following lines of code:

```
<?php print_container_start(true, '', 'header-home'); ?>
  <h1 class="headermain">
    <img src="<?php echo $CFG->themewww .'/'.
    current_theme() ?>/pix/logo.gif" alt="" />
  <?php echo $heading ?></h1>
  <div class="headermenu"><?php echo $menu ?></div>
<?php print_container_end(); ?>
```

3. Replace the following line of code:

```
<?php echo $heading ?>
```

with:

```
<!--<?php echo $heading ?> -->My Front Page Heading
```

as shown below:

```
<?php print_container_start(true, '', 'header-home'); ?>
  <h1 class="headermain">
    <img src="<?php echo $CFG->themewww .'/'.
    current_theme() ?>/pix/logo.gif" alt="" />
<!--<?php echo $heading?> --> My Front Page Heading</h1>
  <div class="headermenu"><?php echo $menu ?></div>
<?php print_container_end(); ?>
```

You can download this code from the Packt website.

4. Save your `header.html` file and refresh your browser window, making sure that you are on your Moodle front page, and you should see something like the following screenshot. Notice that the Moodle heading has now changed to **My Front Page Heading**.

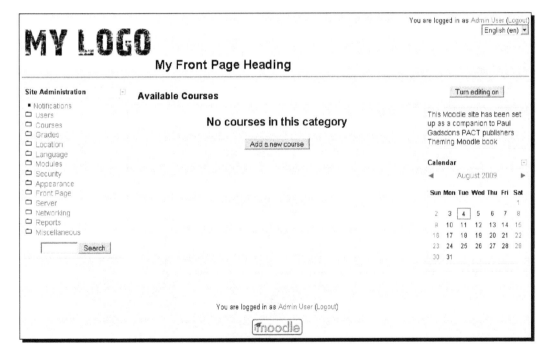

What just happened?

You have just learned how to change the title text on the front page of Moodle. In the process of doing this, you also learned how to comment out PHP code so that you can reuse it at a later stage. It is useful to note here that PHP comments are different than HTML comments. We used an HTML comment here because the PHP code was on only one line and it was self-contained. Hopefully, you have also learned why you might need to do this insofar as you might want to have a different front page for Moodle than you would for the Moodle inner pages.

Most of my Moodle sites, for instance, have no title text on the front page, as I prefer to have a larger graphic logo. Also, I normally prefer to leave the title on the inner pages, as this loads the "course name" when browsing a course.

Customizing the footer

Obviously, the second thing that you are going to do after you have made changes to your Moodle header file is carry on and change the `footer.html` file. The following tasks will be slightly easier than changing the header logo and title text within your Moodle site, as there is much less code and, subsequently, much less to change.

Removing the Moodle logo

The first thing that you will notice about the footer in Moodle is that it has the Moodle logo on the front page of your Moodle site and a **Home** button on all other pages. In addition to this, there is the **login info** text that shows who is logged in and a link to log out.

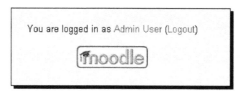

More often than not, Moodle themers will want to remove the Moodle logo so that they can give their Moodle site its own branding. So get stuck in with the next exercise, but don't forget that this logo credits the Moodle community.

Time for action – deleting the Moodle logo

1. Navigate to your `mytheme` directory, right-click on the `footer.html` file, and choose **Open With | WordPad**, as seen below:

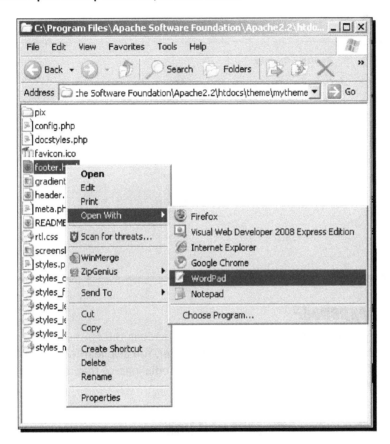

2. Find the following two lines of code:

```
echo $loggedinas;
echo $homelink;
```

3. Comment out the second line using a PHP comment:

```
        echo $loggedinas;
   /*echo $homelink; */
```

4. Save the `footer.html` file and refresh your browser window. You should now see the footer without the Moodle logo, like in the following screenshot:

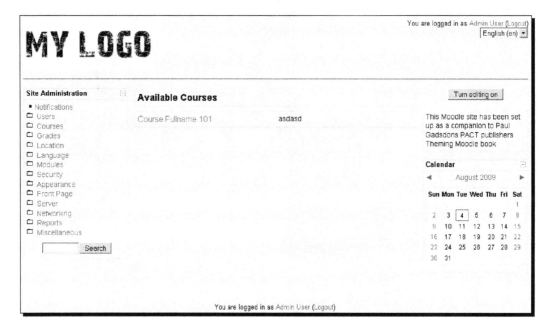

What just happened?

In this exercise, you learned which parts of the PHP code in the `footer.html` file control where the Moodle logo appears in the Moodle footer. You also learned how to comment out the PHP code that controls the rendering of the Moodle logo so that it does not appear. You could try to put the Moodle logo back if you want.

Removing the login info text and link

Now that you have removed the Moodle logo, which of course is completely up to you, you might also want to remove the *login info* link. This link is used exactly like the one in the top right-hand corner of your Moodle site, insofar as it acts as a place where you can log in and log out and provide details of which login you used.

You are logged in as Admin User (Logout)

The only thing to consider here is that if you decide to remove the login info link from the `header.html` file and also remove it from the footer, you will have no easy way of logging in or out of Moodle. It is always wise to leave it either in the header or the footer. You might also consider the advantages of having this here, as some Moodle pages, such as large courses, are very long. So, once the user has scrolled way down the page, he/she has a place to log out if needed.

The following task is very simple and will require you to go through similar steps to the "deleting the logo" exercise. The only difference is that you will comment out a different line of code.

Time for action – deleting the login info text

1. Navigate to your `mytheme` directory, right-click on the `footer.html` file, and choose **Open With | WordPad** (or an editor of your choice), as seen below:

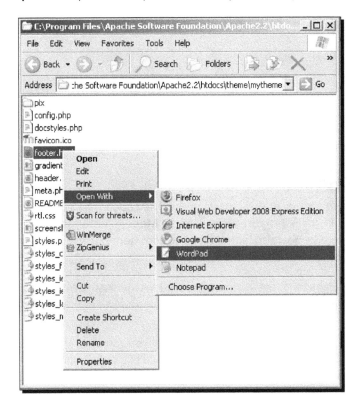

2. Find the following two lines of code:

```
echo $loggedinas;
echo $homelink;
```

3. Comment out the first line by using a PHP comment as shown below:

```
/* echo $loggedinas; */
    echo $homelink;
```

4. Save the `footer.html` file and refresh your browser window. You will see the footer without the Moodle logo or the login info link, as seen in the next screenshot:

What just happened?

In this task, you learned about those parts of the PHP code in the `footer.html` that control whether the Moodle login info text appears in the Moodle footer, similar to the Moodle logo in the previous exercise. You also learned how to comment out the code that controls the rendering of the login info text so that it does not appear.

Have a go hero – adding your own copyright or footer text

The next thing that you are going to do in this chapter is add some custom footer text where the Moodle logo and the login info text were before you removed them. It's completely up to you what to add in the next exercises. If you would like to just add some text to the footer, then please do. However, as part of the following tasks, you are going to add some copyright text and format it using some very basic HTML.

Time for action – adding your own footer text

1. Navigate to your `mytheme` directory, right-click on the `footer.html` file, and choose **Open With | WordPad**.

2. At the very top of the file, paste the following text or choose your own footer text to include: **My School © 2009/10 All rights reserved**, as you can see below.

```
My School &copy; 2009/10 All rights reserved
<?php

    print_container_end(); // content container
```

3. Save the `footer.html` and refresh your browser. You will see that your footer text is at the bottom of the page on the right-hand side. However, this text is aligned to the left as all text in a browser would be.

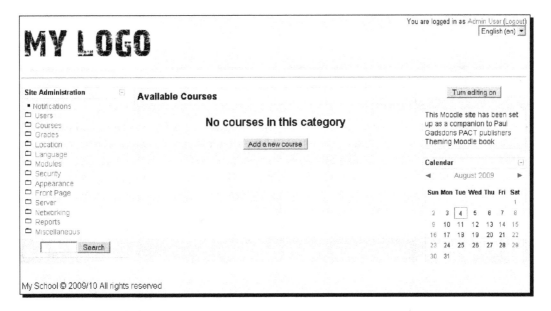

4. Open the `footer.html` file again (if it isn't open already) and wrap the following code around the footer text that you have just added:

```
<div align="right">My School &copy; 2009/10 All rights reserved
</div>
```

5. Save your `footer.html` file and refresh your browser. You will see that the text is now aligned to the right, like in the following screenshot:

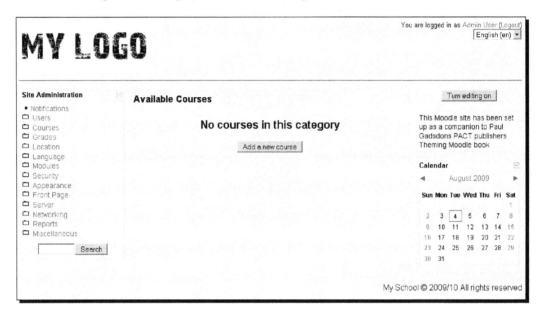

What just happened?

You just added some very basic footer text to your `footer.html` file, saved it, and viewed it in your web browser. You have demonstrated here that it is very easy to add your own text to the `footer.html` file. You have also added some basic HTML formatting to move the text from the left to the right-hand side of the footer. There are other ways to do so, which involve the use of CSS. For instance, you could have given the `<div>` tag a CSS class and used a CSS selector to align the text to the right.

Have a go hero – adding your own footer logo

Now try to see if you can edit the `footer.html` and add the same logo as you have in the `header.html` into the footer. Remember that you can put the logo code anywhere outside of a PHP code block. Try to copy the header logo code and paste it into the `footer.html`. Finally, based on what you have learned, try to align the logo to the right as you did with the footer text.

Browser compatibility – checking whether your changes have worked

As fledgling Moodle themers or website designers, you will need to understand the importance of browser compatibility, which is the need to make sure that your themes or designs all look similar in the many different browsers available in the market.

In most cases, the variation from one browser to another will be minor and probably not even noticeable for the average visitor. But, in some cases, especially when using CSS, you might find that the differences will prevent users from using your Moodle site. The best way to make sure that your site is usable to most of the Internet audience is to test and then test some more.

One of the first things that you will need to do is to find out which browsers are the most commonly used by your visitors. If the Moodle site is an internal educational or corporate site, this will be relatively easy, as your IT department will probably allow only one or two different web browsers to be installed. If, however, your Moodle site is open to public, this task gets a little harder. The best way to see which are the most popular browsers used to visit your Moodle site is to look at your website statistics. By website statistics, I do not mean Moodle's reports, as these will not have the required information; I mean a software package that has been installed on your server such as AWStats, Webalizer, or Google Analytics. Most website-hosting companies will come with a pre-installed website statistics package.

If your organization hosts its own Moodle website, then you will probably need to contact the Moodle server administrator to see if they have any statistics packages installed. If they are not installed, then you could consider installing Google Analytics into Moodle by using the Google Analytics block. Anyway, you will discuss this subject in a little more detail in a while. For now, install Mozilla Firefox and do your first browser compatibility tests.

Obviously, if you already have Mozilla Firefox, then you do not need to install it. If you are already using it, then you could follow the *Time for action – checking whether your changes have worked* section, but replace the testing with Internet Explorer.

Time for action – installing Mozilla Firefox

1. Open your favorite web browser, navigate to Google, and type the following in the search box: **Mozilla Firefox download**. You will be directed to the correct download site for your location.

2. Click on the large **Download** button on the left-hand side. Note that the version number may be different, but the button should otherwise look similar to the one shown below.

3. Choose the **Run** button from the following dialog box:

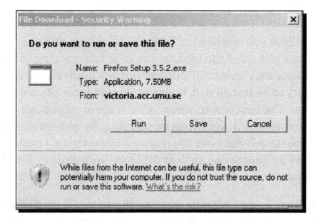

4. After you choose **Run**, the following download dialog box will appear:

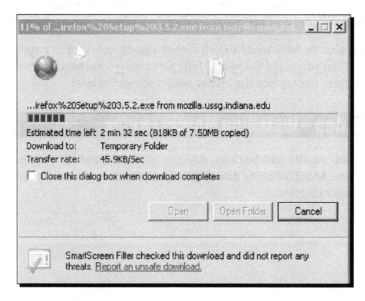

5. After the download has been completed, Windows Internet Explorer will ask you to accept that you want to run this software.

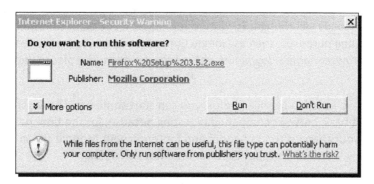

6. Click on **Run** and wait for the **Mozilla Firefox Setup Wizard** to appear.

7. Click on **Next**, choose **Standard Installation, Next** again, and finally, choose **Install**. You now should have a Firefox entry in your start menu and an icon on your desktop.

What just happened?

You have just gone through the steps necessary to install Mozilla Firefox. This process would be the same for most browsers apart from the fact that the website addresses from which you get the downloads will change. For future reference, if you want to install any other browsers for testing purposes, such as Google Chrome or Opera, just go to Google and search for the *browser name - download* where *browser name* is replaced with the actual name.

Now that you have installed Mozilla Firefox, you can start some basic browser compatibility testing. I suggest basic browser compatibility testing because, for the time being, you will only be testing your changes to the header and footer on your Moodle site in two different browsers, namely Windows Internet Explorer and Mozilla Firefox.

Other browsers used to check your changes will be covered at the end of this chapter. Other methods for checking can be used if you don't want to install multiple web browsers on your computer.

Time for action – checking whether your changes have worked

1. Open your Moodle site in Windows Internet Explorer or Mozilla Firefox and log in as the administrator.

2. Open up whichever web browser you haven't already opened, navigate to your Moodle site, and log in again.

3. Now, all you need to do is switch between the two browsers, either by clicking on the tabs of your two browsers on the status bar or pressing *Alt + Tab* keys on your keyboard and choosing either Firefox or Internet Explorer. On the following pages are some screenshots of the two different browsers and what your changes look like:

Mozilla Firefox:

Windows Internet Explorer:

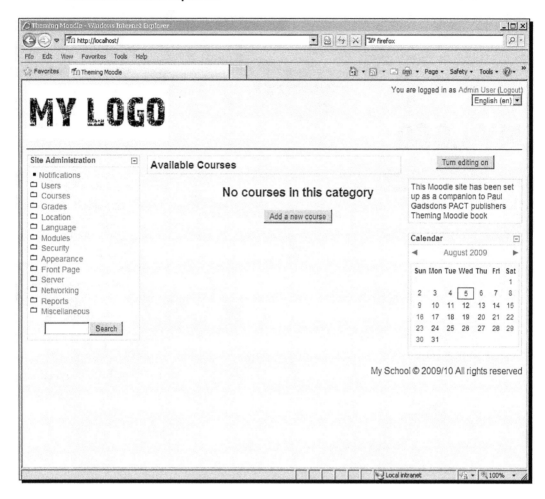

As you can see from your own testing and the preceding screenshots, there are minimal differences between the two browsers. Perhaps you might have been thinking that you would have differences to deal with—well, no. The reason you have done these exercises is to get used to checking every change you make as we go along. This is essential, as it's very easy to forget and do half-a-day's work, only to find that your changes are different in a default browser.

Recommendations

The list of web browsers that are used on the Internet is endless, so you have to be clever about which browsers you use for browser compatibility testing. At the beginning of this chapter, you learned that the best way to see what percentage of users are using a particular browser would be to look at your Moodle site's web server statistics.

The most common web browsers are:

◆ Windows Internet Explorer
◆ Mozilla Firefox
◆ Opera
◆ Safari
◆ Google Chrome

You can download all of these for free and install them. The process would be pretty much the same as downloading Mozilla Firefox.

However, there is a problem here—it is much more difficult to install multiple versions of the same browser. For instance, you might want to have Windows Internet Explorer 5.0, 6.0, 7.0, and 8.0, because all these versions of the same web browser will render web pages and interpret CSS rules in slightly different ways. The only real way around this is to use an emulator or website service to check for web browser compatibility across different versions of the same browser.

The best by far that I have managed to find is the free "Browsershots" service found at `http://browsershots.org`. All you need to do is enter the URL of your Moodle site (assuming it's on the Internet), and check or uncheck the browsers you want to see with your Moodle site in them. A note of warning here: only check the most common browsers; try to avoid checking all of the boxes on this page, as the service takes between 15 minutes and a couple of hours to take screenshots and upload them to your account.

For instance, I have Firefox, Internet Explorer, Opera, Safari, and Google Chrome installed on my PC, which I use for browser compatibility testing. If I need to see whether there are any differences in the look and layout of my Moodle theme across multiple versions of the same browser, then I will use the above service.

In addition to the various online tools available for browser compatibility testing, there is also a tool called **Microsoft Expression Web SuperPreview**, which is a useful tool that allows developers to debug websites between all of the different versions of Internet Explorer.

You may wish to have a look at these online services as well:

- Xenocode Browser Sandbox
- CrossBrowserTesting.com
- BrowsrCamp
- Litmus

A full list of the online services will be included in the appendix.

Have a go hero - downloading Google Chrome

Go and do a Google search for the Google Chrome browser download. Navigate to the correct page and see if you can download, run, and install the Google Chrome browser. The process should be similar to what you have already learned in the *Installing Mozilla Firefox* section.

Pop quiz – doing the thing

Q1. Why are there two pieces of title code in the header.html file?

- A. So that you can cut and paste it
- B. Because Moodle loads a different header on the front page and on the inner pages
- C. To make double sure that it loads correctly

Q2. What would you do to make a piece of code unused?

- A. Delete it
- B. Put a comment around it
- C. Move it to the bottom of the file

Q3. What is the correct format to comment out code in a PHP file?

- A. //* my comment//*
- B. */my comment/*
- C. /* my comment*/

Summary

Throughout this chapter, you have learned about making basic changes to the header and footer HTML files for your Moodle theme. You have learned that it's relatively easy to make small changes such as replacing the Moodle logo with your own. You have also learned about the importance of checking your changes in several web browsers and how to download and install different web browsers as part of the testing process. Finally, you learned how to check that your changes have been applied by using online services such as Browsershots.

Specifically, we covered:

- How to add your own logo to your theme's `header.html` file
- How to remove the Moodle logo and login info link in the `footer.html` file
- How and why it is important to test these changes in different browsers
- How to download other web browsers
- How to comment out HTML and PHP code

Now that you've learned about editing the header and footers in your Moodle theme, we will move on to the next chapter to learn about Cascading Style Sheets (CSS) and their relationship with Moodle. You will then use the CSS files within your Moodle theme directory to change the default fonts, colors, backgrounds, and link styles before finishing on Moodle and the importance of accessibility.

4
Adjusting the Colors and Fonts

In this chapter, we will initially cover what Cascading Style Sheets (CSS) are and why stylesheets are important when theming Moodle. After this, you will change the default font, set the font size and color, set the link color, and change the background color by using CSS. Additionally, you will learn about the concept of "accessibility" so that you can theme Moodle from the outset with accessibility in mind. Finally, we will briefly discuss what we have learned in this chapter.

Here we shall cover:

◆ What cascading style sheets are

◆ How Moodle makes use of CSS

◆ How to set the default font

◆ How to set the font color and font size

◆ How to set the link color

◆ How to change the background color

◆ What accessibility is and why it is important

So, let's get on with it...

Important preliminary points

In order for you to work your way through this chapter, it is highly recommended that you download Mozilla Firefox, which is simply a better developer's web browser. In the last chapter, you likely installed the Firefox browser, but if not, you are encouraged to do so now in order to be ready to complete the activities in this chapter.

Installing Firebug and the Web Developer Toolbar

There are hundreds of free extensions available for the Firefox browser. Two of the most useful extensions that concern Moodle theming are the **Web Developer Toolbar** and **Firebug**; these extensions will allow you to inspect the HTML code and CSS in detail without having to open the original file. They also provide an astounding array of functionality that makes most web developers and Moodle themers wonder how they ever managed without them. For example, using either of these extensions will allow you to temporarily make a change to the CSS code without having to modify the CSS code file.

So, for this chapter, you will download Firebug to help us work with Moodle's CSS and make the required changes. It can't be emphasized enough how important these Firefox extensions are to the budding Moodle themer. Moodle uses multiple CSS that inherit each other's style declarations. This makes it challenging to follow the cascading effect and accurately change most of its styles without the help of Firebug or the Web Developer Toolbar.

Time for action – installing the Firebug extension for Firefox

1. Open Mozilla Firefox and on the menu bar click on **Tools | Add-ons** as shown below:

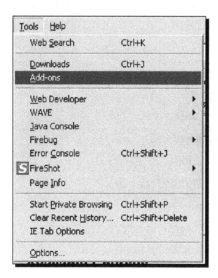

2. You should see the following dialog box of recommended Add-ons. Note that the contents may vary from this image.

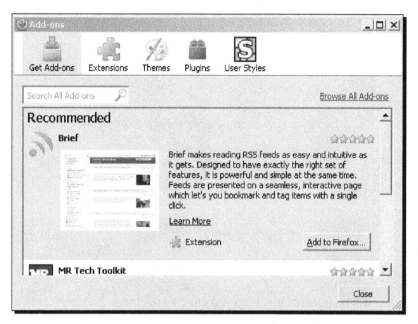

3. Ignore the recommended Add-ons and click on the link on the top right-hand corner: **Browse All Add-ons**. This will open up the main Firefox extension website.

4. Type the word **Firebug** in the main search box at the top of the page and press the *Enter/Return* key on your keyboard.

5. The very top search result will be the Firebug extension. Click on the **Add to Firefox** button on the right-hand side.

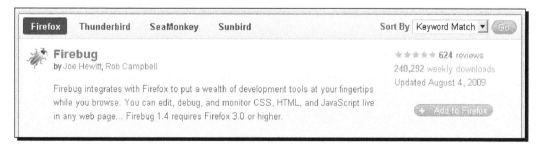

6. The following dialog box will appear. Click on the **Install Now** button.

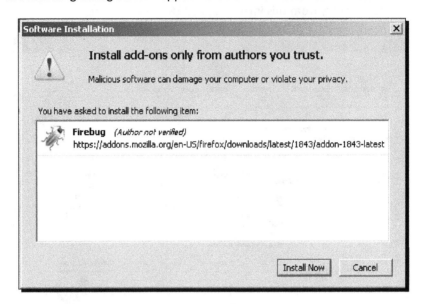

7. Firebug will be installed and then you will be asked to restart Firefox. Click on the **Restart Firefox** button and wait for Firefox to restart.

Top Tip – Do not install too many Add-ons

There are thousands of Firefox Add-ons available for us to download, but it is very important not to get carried away and download hundreds of them. The more you have, the slower Firefox will work, so try to be conservative with your choices. But by all means please do have a look at the popular ones and install a few, as this will make you more familiar with the installation process.

8. Now repeat this exercise but search for the Web Developer Toolbar and install this as well.

What just happened?

You have just learned how to install a Firefox Add-on by using the **Add-ons** functionality from Firefox's **Tools** menu. Another option is to navigate to the Firefox extensions website and install them from there. Just do a Google search for Firefox Add-ons.

Cascading Style Sheets and Moodle

Before you continue and start to change the fonts, typeface, size, and colors of a Moodle theme, it is important to understand a little about CSS and how they are used in a Moodle theme.

CSS were first developed in the mid 1990s as an attempt to separate the content of a document from its design. In the past, web pages were written almost exclusively by using HTML, and only a single document to describe both the structure and design style of the web page was built. This was far from the ideal because it meant that for every web page built, its design markup had to be repeated over and over again.

The introduction of CSS was slow but it's now commonplace. CSS is used as a way of separating the stylistic elements from the content and therefore provides stylistic instructions to HTML and XHTML documents.

CSS can therefore define all of the stylistic parts of a web page, referencing them by tag type, such as Class or ID. CSS can be used to control the size, color, position, and visibility of almost any design element on the page, such as fonts, tables, borders, and backgrounds.

Moodle uses CSS extensively throughout and relies on the CSS ability to inherit its rules from other stylesheets (Cascading).The inheritance in CSS is the way that elements that don't already have predefined styles will take on the styles of their parents in the document tree. In other words, the parent styles set out in the top-most CSS will be overwritten by the same styles written in a child stylesheet.

As we will be making only small changes to our copied `standard` theme, namely `mytheme` (created in *Chapter 2, Moodle Theming*), it is best at this stage to create our own stylesheet and ask the `config.php` file in the root of our `mytheme` folder to reference it. We can then copy styles from the standard set of stylesheets and paste them into our new stylesheet.

We'll cover more on CSS a little later, but for now, you will make a new stylesheet and ask the `config.php` file to reference it.

Time for action – creating a new Cascading Style Sheet

1. Navigate to `C:\Program Files\Apache Software Foundation\Apache 2.2\htdocs\themes\mytheme`.

2. Right-click on some empty space and choose **New | Text Document**, as seen in the following screenshot:

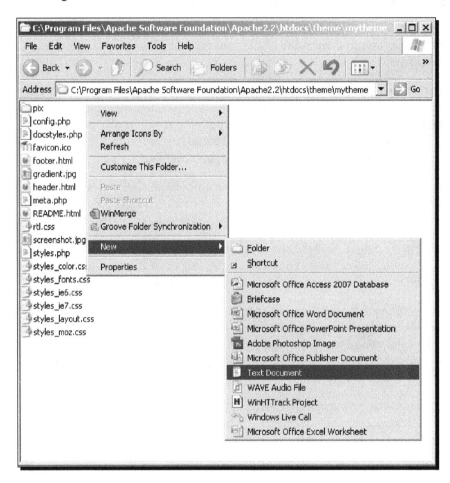

3. Rename the `New Text Document.txt` file to `my_style.css`.

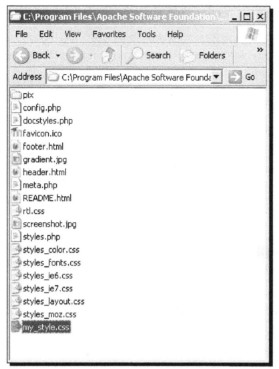

4. Right-click on the `config.php` file in the same directory and choose **Open With | WordPad** and look for the following line:

```
$THEME->sheets = array('styles_layoutffvv', 'styles_fonts',
                       'styles_color');
```

5. Change this line to:

```
$THEME->sheets = array('styles_layout', 'styles_fonts',
                       'styles_color', 'my_style');
```

You can download this code from the Packt website.

6. Remember to leave out the `.css` extension on the filename—this is necessary for the `config.php` file to be parsed by the PHP processor.

7. Save and close the `config.php` file.

What just happened?

In the last exercise, you set up Moodle to use your own newly defined stylesheet (`my_style.css`), so you can now make some changes to the CSS. You added a new stylesheet to your `mytheme config` file and created that stylesheet. You did this so that any changes that you make will not interfere with the standard theme that your *mytheme* is based upon.

Changing the default font

One of the first tasks when altering a Moodle theme by editing its CSS is to change the default font, which is used throughout your Moodle site. You are going to do this not so much because your *mytheme* theme uses the wrong font, but just to learn how and why you would want to do this. But please beware that many institutions have a specific font for branding purposes. In the exercises for this chapter, you will change this several times so that you can get used to the process.

Time for action – changing the default font by using Firebug

1. Open your Moodle site in Mozilla Firefox by navigating to `http://localhost` (assuming that you are working on a local Moodle site). If not, just type in the URL of the Moodle site with which you are working.

2. Log in by clicking on the **Login** link in the top right-hand corner.

3. Look at the status bar of Firefox on the bottom right-hand side and you should notice a small beetle icon, as seen below:

Alternatively press the *F12* key on your keyboard.

4. Click on the beetle icon and the Firebug Add-on, which you installed earlier, will open and look something like the following screenshot:

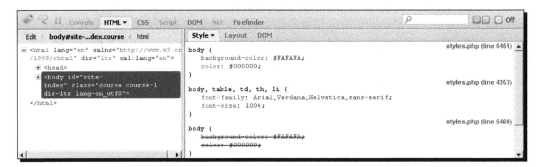

5. On the top left-hand side of Firebug there is a small icon used to inspect elements on the web page; click on this:

6. Roll your mouse around the page and you should see a blue border outline on every page element over which you hover your mouse. You should be able to see the HTML in the left-hand window change to show you the HTML you have hovered over and the CSS (right-hand) for the hovered area in the window on the side.

7. Click once on the text, **No courses in this category**, which is directly in the middle of your Moodle site and can be seen below. This freezes Firebug, so you can inspect the CSS or HTML of that element.

No courses in this category

8. Scroll down the CSS (right-hand) window until you see the body class:

```
body, table, td, th, li {
font-family:Arial,Verdana,Helvetica,sans-serif;
font-size:100%;
}
```

9. Replace the word `Arial` with `Comic Sans MS`.

10. You can do this simply by clicking on the text in the window and overwriting what is there already.

11. Press the *Enter/Return* key and view the change as you do it. You should see that the middle text that you inspected earlier has changed to Comic Sans MS. You might also have noticed that all the text on your Moodle site has changed to this font. This is because you have temporarily changed the main font that has been set through CSS onto the body class.

No courses in this category

What just happened?

What you have just done in the last task is learn how to use Firebug to inspect an element on your Moodle web page. You have learned that it is relatively simple to roll your mouse over different elements on the page and see what CSS is associated with it in the left-hand window of Firebug. You have also learned that you can change the CSS visible in Firebug by typing straight into it and viewing the changes as you make them. Remember, though, these are only temporary changes and will be reset as soon as you refresh your browser window or close Firebug.

More on Firebug

You might have noticed in the last exercise that the style you changed was not the first style on the list. You might also have been asking yourself, "how do I know which style to choose?" Well, some of this comes with experience, as I already know that most websites use the body class to define the default font throughout the site; you may have known this as well.

Most often, you will have an idea of what you are looking for. In this case, you were looking for a font selector. You needed to know which class was controlling the font throughout your Moodle site. So, the first font selector you saw was the one at the top of the cascade.

Firebug has a clever way of telling you whether a selector is being used or not. It simply strikes through the ones that are not active for that particular element.

One last thing to note here is that Firebug is an inspector and an editor insofar as you can make changes on the fly, so you can see the resultant changes in the browser. However, it will not save these changes directly to the stylesheets, so the changes that we made earlier will be gone once we refresh our web browser.

For the next exercise, you need to find the body CSS selector again and copy it into your new stylesheet that you made earlier. It will the override the standard body CSS selector and use your body selector to control the default font.

Time for action – making our changes permanent

1. Repeat the first seven steps of the previous exercise.

2. Scroll down the CSS (right-hand) window until you see the body selector. Copy it by highlighting the whole selector, as seen below, and then right-clicking and choosing **Copy.**

```
body, table, td, th, li {
    font-family: Arial,Verdana,Helvetica,sans-serif;
    font-size: 80%;
}
```

3. Navigate to your my_styles.css file that you created earlier in C:\Program Files\Apache Software Foundation\Apache 2.2\htdocs\themes\ mytheme. Open this file by right-clicking and choosing **Open With | WordPad**.

4. Paste the CSS selector that you should have on your clipboard into this empty file.

5. Change the Arial font to Comic Sans MS and save the file.

6. Go back to your web browser and press the *F5* key. As you can see below, you have now made the change to the body selector in the *mytheme* theme permanent without changing any CSS from the standard theme—the original *standard* theme has not been altered in any way.

What just happened?

You have just learned how to make your CSS changes permanent by using Firebug. You learned how to copy CSS selectors from Firebug into another stylesheet that you made at an earlier stage. You have learned that by doing this, you have overridden the styles already applied to this document by the styles in the `copy of the standard` theme.

If you hadn't used Firebug, you would have had to search through all of the other four stylesheets that came with the standard theme until you found the right one. That's not too bad if it's an easy one such as the body selector, but if it was the one where you didn't know the selector's name, then it would have been almost impossible. For example, when using Firebug, it clearly displays all of the possible selectors and strikes through any that are not active. This makes it much easier for you to know which one is being used and from which stylesheet it comes.

Setting the font color and size

The next thing that you may want to do is to change the colors and sizes of the default fonts that are used throughout the site. The next set of exercises has just been designed so that you can get used to the process of changing the font color and font size elements via CSS. Oh, and by the way, if you want you can go back and change the default font to Verdana or Tahoma, as these are much better fonts than Comic Sans MS because they are easier to read and look more professional. You used the Comic Sans MS font in the previous example because the change is easily seen.

So, let's get on with the next set of changes...

Time for action – changing the font color

1. Open your Moodle site in Mozilla Firefox by navigating to `http://localhost`.

2. Log in by clicking on the **Login** link in the top right-hand corner.

3. Open your `my_style.css` file that you created earlier by navigating to `C:\Program Files\Apache Software Foundation\Apache 2.2\ htdocs\ themes\mytheme`.

4. There should be only one selector in this file namely `body`—the one that we added earlier. You need to make one change here, just add `color:red;` in the end as follows:

```
body, table, td, th, li {
font-family:comic sans ms,Verdana,Helvetica,sans-serif;
font-size:100%;
color:red;
}
```

5. Save and close `my_style.css` and go back and refresh your browser. You will see that most of the fonts have changed to red.

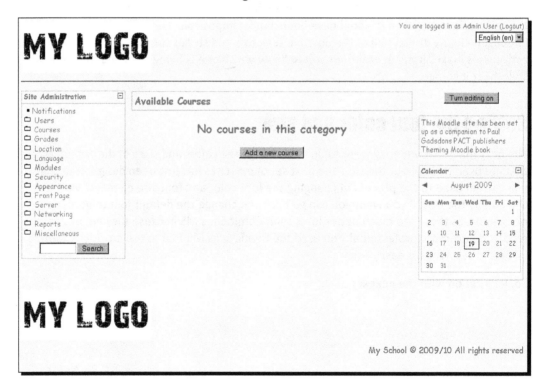

What just happened?

In this task, you have made a simple change to the color of the default font used with your Moodle theme. You have done this using what you completed in the previous exercise by simply adding a color selector to `my_style.css` and the already created CSS body class.

You have probably noticed that not all of the text has changed and that there are still quite a lot of blue fonts scattered around the page. This is due to the fact that the leftover blue fonts are HTML links and these have a completely different set of CSS classes, namely `a:link, a:active, a:visited`, and `a:hover`.

Changing the default font size

Another task that you may want to do is to change the default font size. You may wish, for instance, to make all the fonts larger so that people who have visual disabilities will be able to better see the text on your Moodle site.

Time for action – setting the font size

1. Open up the *mytheme* theme's `my_style.css` file with WordPad.

2. Look for the line: `font-size:100%` and change it to `110%`.

3. Save and close your `my_style.css` file.

4. Go back to your web browser and refresh the page. You should see that all the text on the page, including the links, has gotten larger.

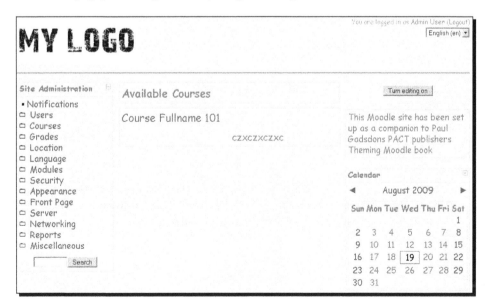

What just happened?

In this exercise, you have learned to increase the default font size across the whole site. Of course, this was only an example, and I would probably recommend that you should put this back to as it was, for now.

Setting the link colors

In this next section, we will be digging a little deeper into Moodle's CSS and you will be learning how to change the link colors throughout the site. Links are slightly trickier than the normal text, as they have several different CSS selectors. For example, a link has different selectors for its normal (unvisited) state, its visited state (once someone has clicked on it), and what it should look like when your mouse is hovering over it (hover state). These also have a correct order, which is important, because if the order is set wrong, some web browsers may not render your links as you want them. This is the correct order:

1. `a:link`
2. `a:visited`
3. `a:hover`
4. `a:active`

Time for action – changing the link colors

1. Open your web browser and browse to your Moodle site.

2. Open Firebug by clicking on the Firebug icon or by pressing the *F12* key.

3. Click on the inspect icon and roll your mouse over one of the site administration links.

4. Copy the second CSS class and paste it in your `my_style.css` file (under the `body` class).

   ```
   a:link, a:visited {
   color:#0000FF;
   }
   ```

5. Change the `color: #0000FF;` to `#000000;` —the former is the standard blue link and the latter is black. Save your `my_style.css` file and refresh your browser. All the links (visited and unvisited) should now be black.

Please note: I wouldn't ordinarily advise people to have the same color for their link and visited link selectors because this can detract from the normal functionality of the link selectors. It is a useful feature to have different colors for these selectors because the users can easily identify where they have been, as the links change color once they are clicked.

6. Following on from what you have just done, change the link hover color so that when your mouse rolls over the link, you have a different color. Follow the first three steps of this exercise and then look for the second selector; this one will be a hover selector:

```
a:hover {
color:#FF0000;
}
```

7. Copy this class and paste it in your `my_style.css` file.

8. Change the line: `color:#FF0000` to `color:#336600`.

9. Save your `my_style.css` file and refresh your browser. You should now see that your link hover color has changed to green.

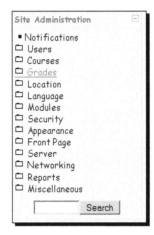

What just happened?

You have learned to change the default link color and link hover color by copying the link selectors from Firebug and pasting them into your `my_style.css` file.

Easy, wasn't it?

Changing the background

The final change that you are going to make with regard to your Moodle theme in this chapter is to change the background color of the site. There will be two exercises in this section: one will be to simply change the color and the other will be to use a background image to spice up your design a little.

So, let's get on with it....

Time for action – changing the background color

1. Open the *mytheme* theme's `my_style.css` file, if not already open.

2. Look for the body class at the top:

```
body, table, td, th, li {
font-family:comic sans ms,Verdana,Helvetica,sans-serif;
font-size:100%;
color:red;
}
```

3. Change it to:

```
body, table, td, th, li {
font-family:comic sans ms,Verdana,Helvetica,sans-serif;
font-size:100%;
color:red;
background-color:grey;
}
```

You can download this code from the Packt website.

4. Save your `my_style.css` file and refresh your browser.

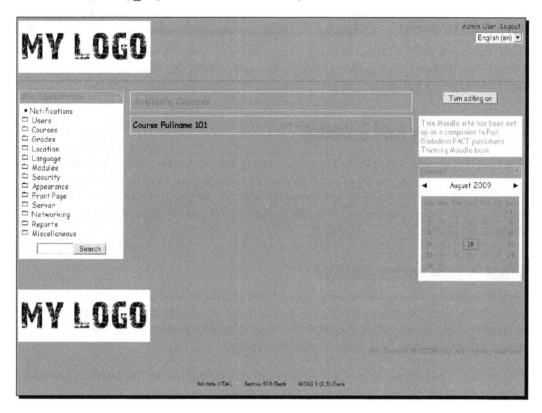

As you can see in the above screenshot from the previous task, the background has changed to the color that we wanted, namely gray, however, the sideblocks haven't. This is because they have their own CSS classes, so we can set these to a different color, if required.

Now, let's try to add a background image.

What just happened?

In the last exercise, you learned how to change the background color of your Moodle site. In the process, you discovered that the sideblocks in Moodle have their own CSS classes and subsequently will not change when setting the page or site-wide background color using CSS.

Have a go hero – change the background and font color and font type

Let's see if we have accomplished our goals for this chapter. Go back and remove the background image and replace this with the color white as it was before. Then, change the font back to the color black and set display to Verdana instead of Comic Sans MS.

Have a go hero – change the background color of the sideblocks

Right, this one is slightly harder because you are going to have to use Firebug to find the correct style that you need to change the background color of the right- and left-hand blocks. Change the background of these blocks to the following color: #f1f1f1

Accessibility and Moodle

The final section of this chapter will introduce you to the issues surrounding web accessibility and how to ensure that you do as much as you can to make your Moodle themes more accessible. Because you are likely to be working in or for the education sector, it is imperative that you try to make sure that as many different groups of people as possible have access to your Moodle sites.

What is web accessibility?

Web accessibility means making websites and web applications as usable as possible for people with disabilities. More specifically, it means that we should make our websites accessible to people who have disabilities that can restrict them in terms of the ability to understand, navigate, and interact with the website.

This includes older people who might not have an actual disability per se, but have suffered from the changing abilities that are associated with age.

Web accessibility includes all of the disabilities that affect how people use the Web, including visual, auditory, speech, physical, and neurological disabilities.

Over a period of time, the Web has become an increasingly important communication and resource tool for everyday life. This is because ensuring that the Web is accessible has been considered essential in terms of equal access and equal opportunity for people with disabilities. Many countries now have legislation in place that ensures that the Web is made accessible to all, so please be mindful of this when creating Moodle themes. It is also particularly frowned upon to not consider all who use these services in the context of social education.

Moodle and web accessibility

Over the years, Moodle has improved and has been made more and more accessible, and this will likely continue. However, because Moodle uses themes that can be built by its users, there are some instances where Moodle can fail in terms of accessibility. The HTML editor in Moodle, for instance, doesn't necessarily fail any accessibility tests, but it can create issues because it allows untrained users to create their own HTML sections (web pages). In these terms, users could create materials that are not accessible or do not conform to an institution's web accessibility guidelines.

An example of this is that Moodle itself, without any course materials, does conform to most countries' web accessibility guidelines or rules. Once the course materials are added, then there is no guarantee that these rules or guidelines will be met. This is because most web users are not aware of the importance or impact of these rules and therefore do not have sufficient skills to ensure that they are met.

Something very simple such as leaving out an `ALT` tag on an image creates a situation where people with visual disabilities will not know what the image represents. Another such issue is users uploading course material in only one format, such as PDF files or by using Adobe Flash. Although these formats can be made accessible, they are not likely to be created and uploaded by untrained users.

It's for these reasons that institutions using Moodle will need to implement proper training programs for its staff to ensure that Moodle remains accessible to all those who want to use it.

What does this mean to us?

Well, as we are the Moodle administrators, we will probably be partly responsible for the platform as a whole and therefore, will be actively involved in issues such as these. We will probably be asked to create courses within Moodle that teach the fundamentals of web accessibility and keep a close eye on which activities and resources users use as they create their Moodle courses.

Does this affect the theming process?

Yes it does, as we can easily forget to check our theme changes against web accessibility guidelines and possibly render our organization liable under the law! We can also create themes that help people with disabilities access and use our Moodle sites. For instance, high contrast themes help people with visual disabilities see links and text easier.

What can we do to ensure that our themes and Moodle sites are accessible?

The best thing to do is to check your themes against one of the many web accessibility checking services available on the Web or through the use of toolbars for your favorite web browsers. In fact, if you installed the Web Developer Toolbar at the start of this chapter, you already have the ability to do some basic checking. Following is a list of such services and also a few general accessibility reference sites for you to learn more about this subject. Also, your organization probably already has someone trained in accessibility standards, so there is no need to panic.

Online Web Accessibility testers

http://www.cynthiasays.com/

Tools

Web Developer Toolbar - Firefox

https://addons.mozilla.org/en-US/firefox/addon/60

WCAG contrast checker - Firefox

https://addons.mozilla.org/en-US/firefox/addon/7391

Firefox accessibility extension

https://addons.mozilla.org/en-US/firefox/addon/5809

AIS Web Accessibility Toolbar - Internet Explorer

http://www.visionaustralia.org.au/ais/toolbar/

Reference Sites

Web Accessibility imitative

http://www.w3.org/WAI/

Web Content Accessibility Guidelines (WCAG) Overview

http://www.w3.org/WAI/intro/wcag.php

Pop quiz

Q1. Why do we use WordPad instead of notepad to edit HTML and CSS files?

    A. Because it is smaller.

    B. Because it is free.

    C Because it retains the original formatting.

Q2. What makes Mozilla Firefox a great web browser for a Moodle themer?

    A. It looks much better.

    B. It has hundreds of free extensions.

    C. It is quick to download.

    D. It's free.

Q3. If we want to change the style when we roll the mouse over a link what CSS selector should we change?

    A. `a:link`

    B. `a:visited`

    C. `a:hover`

    D. `a:active`

Have a go hero – add a border to the blocks

Okay, we have to assume that you have managed to do the last task and that your blocks have a nice gray background. Now, you should try to add a slightly gray border around these blocks; use the color specified below. I have included the selector in case you didn't know:

```
border-color:#dddddd;
```

Have a go hero – customize the block header

In this exercise, you will be adding the same color background as the blocks but this time to the block header. You will need to use Firebug to find the right style. After you have done this, I want you to change the height of the header to 16px and use the following padding:

```
min-height:16px;
padding:6px 7px 6px 9px;
```

Your Moodle site should look like this:

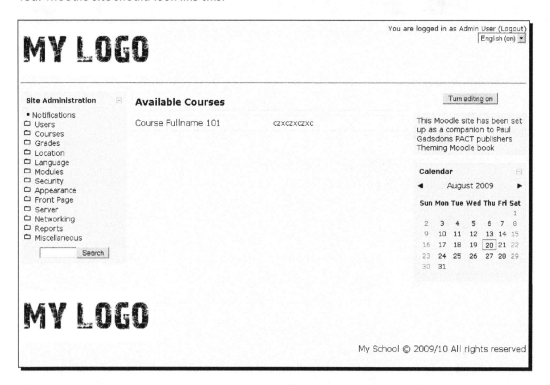

Have a go hero – browser compatibility

Now go and check that the changes that you have made throughout this chapter have worked in Internet Explorer and perhaps even Google Chrome. By way of reminder, it is recommended to check your changes when you make them in multiple browsers to ensure that you are getting the desired look regardless of which browser your users use.

Summary

To summarize, in this chapter you have learned how to install Firefox Add-ons to greatly improve the functionality of the browser in terms of web development. You have learned how to create a new CSS. You have also learned how and why you use our own CSS rather than edit the current files from your theme directory. You now understand how to set Moodle's `config` file to pick up any additional stylesheets that you might use and understand more about Moodle's theming process.

You have learned how to change some of the common elements on our Moodle site by using CSS. You have explored the concept of web accessibility and why accessibility issues are important.

Specifically, we covered:

- Installing Firebug and the Web Developer Toolbar
- Cascading Style Sheets (CSS) and Moodle
- Changing the default font
- Setting the font color and font size
- Setting the link colors (unvisited, visited, and hover)
- Changing the background (color and/or image)
- Accessibility in the Moodle environment

Now that you've learned about making basic changes to your Moodle theme, we will move onto the next chapter to learn about making changes to the layout of Moodle using CSS. You will learn how to set the width of a Moodle site and learn the differences between fixed and liquid designs. Carrying on from this, you will learn how to set the block widths and what impact such changes might have when using different screen sizes.

5
Changing the Layout

In this chapter, you will be changing the default layout of Moodle through the use of CSS. You will learn how to set the width of the Moodle site and understand the differences between fixed and liquid Moodle theme designs. You will then move on to learn how to change the width of the sideblocks and introduce resolution-independent design concepts when you work through the exercises. Finally, we will briefly discuss what we have learned in this chapter.

Here we shall cover:

◆ The differences between full (liquid) screen and fixed width themes
◆ Different screen sizes and Moodle theming
◆ Setting Moodle's width
◆ Changing the left and right blocks' column widths

So, let's get on with it...

Full screen versus reduced width theme

It's easy to assume that all Moodle sites fill the whole screen when opened and that this is the only format that we can have when theming a Moodle website. This is generally because most Moodle sites do use the whole screen (liquid) when they are being used as course management systems due to a restricted amount of space for content available to reduced width designs (fixed). However, in some cases and especially when companies or institutions want their Moodle site to match their current corporate website's design, they would prefer to use a reduced width design.

There are some prebuilt and downloadable reduced width themes for you to use if you require. Have a look at one of them so that you can see the difference.

Time for action – choosing a reduced (fixed) width theme

1. Open your web browser (if not already open) and navigate to your local Moodle site.

2. Log in as the administrator.

3. Navigate to **Appearance | Themes | Theme Selector**.

4. If you scroll down the list of themes, you will see that there aren't any reduced (fixed) themes installed by default. Subsequently, you will need to connect to the Internet and navigate to Moodle to find one.

5. To do this, open another tab or browser window and navigate to `http://moodle.org/mod/data/view.php?id=6552`; this should bring you to Moodle's theme database.

6. Locate the *ability to learn* theme, as seen below, (you might need to search for this, as there are a lot of themes in the Moodle database) and click on the **Download** link.

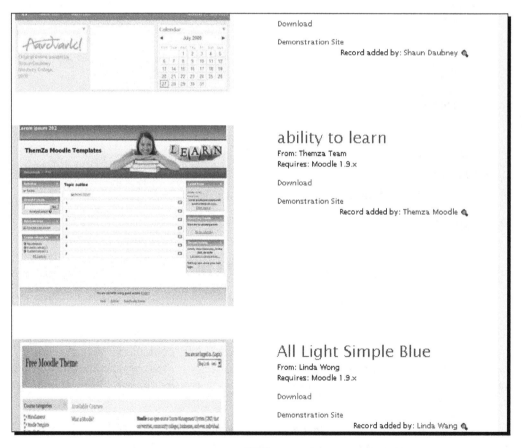

7. Save the `ability-to-learn.zip` file to your desktop.

8. Right-click on the `ability-to-learn.zip` file and choose **ZipGenius | Extract here, to ability-to-learn**.

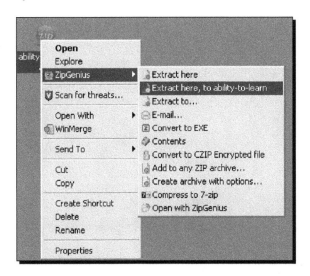

9. Double-click on the `ability-to-learn` folder and copy the `ability-to-learn` folder within it by right-clicking on it and choosing **Copy**, as seen below.

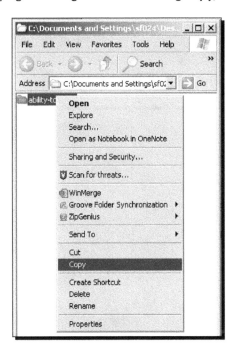

10. Navigate to your main Moodle site's `theme` directory, right-click on it, and choose **Paste**. This should copy your *ability to learn* theme to your `theme` directory, making it ready for you to use.

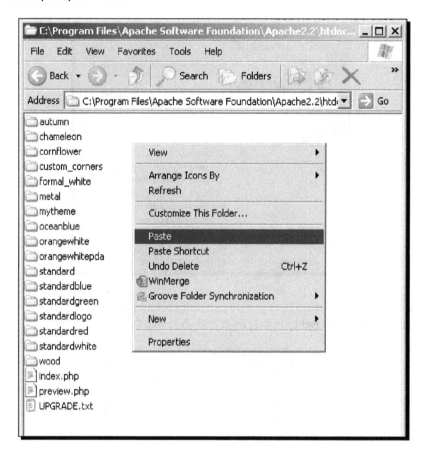

11. Open your web browser and navigate to **Site Administration | Appearance | Themes | Theme Selector** and, at the very top of the page, you should see the *ability to learn* theme. Then, just click on the **Choose** button.

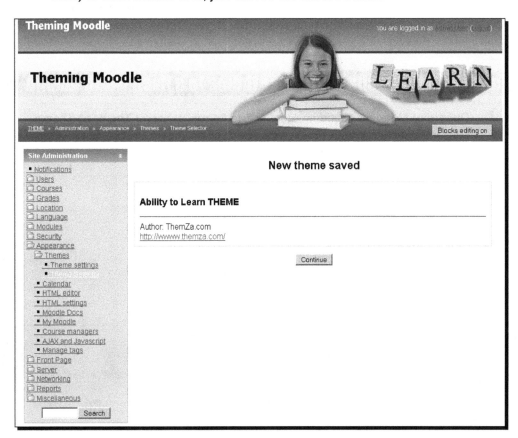

What just happened?

You have just downloaded a fixed width Moodle theme from the main `Moodle.org` website and have copied it to your local theme's folder. You then set Moodle to load this theme as an example so that you can see the difference between full screen (liquid) designs and reduced width (fixed) theme designs.

At this stage, it would be worth having a good look at the differences between this type of theme and the standard theme that you have been customizing. In particular, try to resize the browser window by using the *ability to learn* theme. You will notice that every element on the page has the same width because it is a fixed design and not liquid. The blocks and whitespace do not get any smaller or larger. Now, if you go back to your *mytheme* theme and do the same, most of the whitespace on the theme will resize as you make the browser window smaller.

Setting a theme's width

Now that you have looked at a fixed width theme, have a go at changing your *mytheme* so that it fills only the central part of the browser window. I probably would not recommend reducing the center column's width on a production server because of space constraints within courses. However, it is a good exercise to get used to changing the layout of Moodle.

Time for action – changing your theme to a fixed width design

1. Open your Moodle site and navigate to **Site Administration | Themes | Theme Selector** and change your theme from *ability to learn* back to your *mytheme*. You should see something similar to the following screenshot:

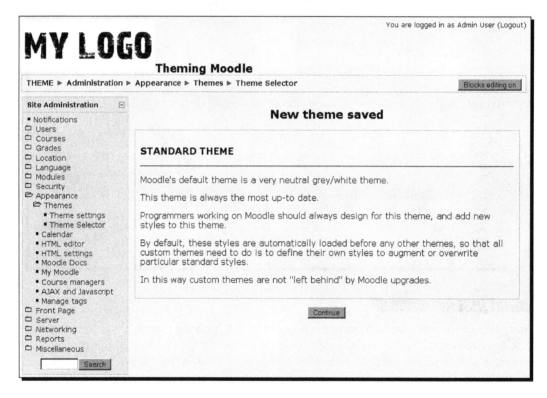

You now need to add a `page` class to your `user_styles.css` file so that you can control the width of your Moodle site. This class is defined in the HTML of your Moodle site, so all you need to do is to add it to your `user_styles.css` file.

2. Now, navigate to your `mytheme` directory in your local Moodle folder and right-click on `mystyle.css` and choose **Open With | WordPad** or your preferred text editor. If you are using Windows, remember that your `mytheme` directory is in the `C:\Program Files\Apache Software Foundation\Apache 2.2\htdocs\theme` directory. Your CSS file should be the same as the next screenshot:

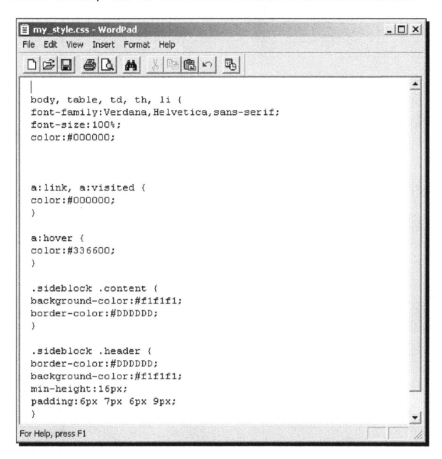

3. Add the following lines of CSS code to this file just under the `body` class and save it.

```css
#page {
    width:975px;
    margin:0px auto;
    background: #ffffff;
}
```

This is the CSS code that forces the page to be 975 pixels wide and therefore forces your theme to be fixed.

Your my_style.css file should look like the following screenshot:

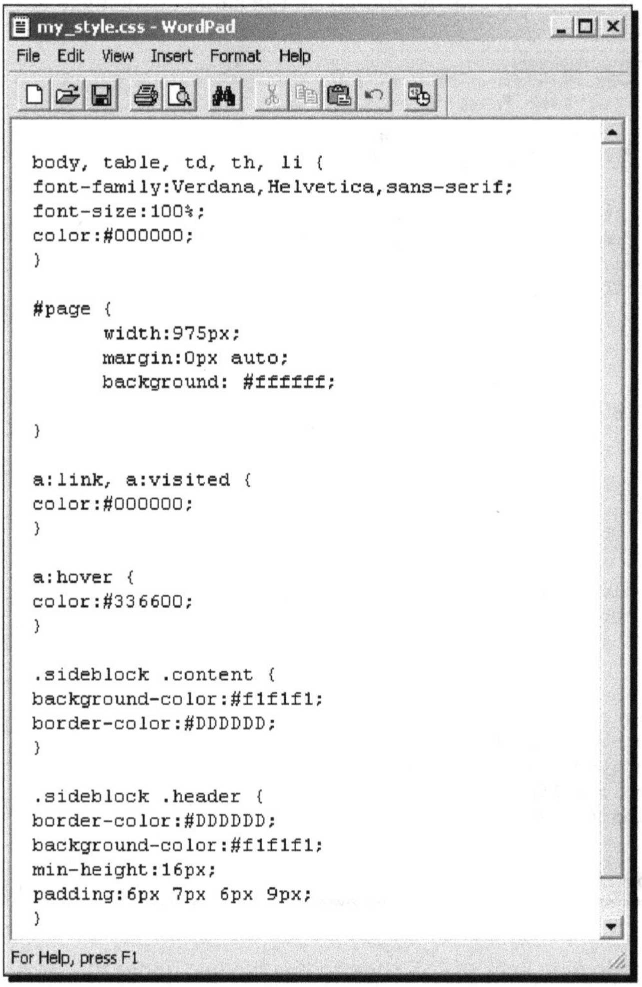

```
body, table, td, th, li {
font-family:Verdana,Helvetica,sans-serif;
font-size:100%;
color:#000000;
}

#page {
        width:975px;
        margin:0px auto;
        background: #ffffff;

}

a:link, a:visited {
color:#000000;
}

a:hover {
color:#336600;
}

.sideblock .content {
background-color:#f1f1f1;
border-color:#DDDDDD;
}

.sideblock .header {
border-color:#DDDDDD;
background-color:#f1f1f1;
min-height:16px;
padding:6px 7px 6px 9px;
}
```

4. Open your web browser and if you are not already at your local Moodle site, navigate there, and press the *F5* key or hit refresh. You should see something similar to the following screenshot. Notice that the main page isn't as wide as it was and has been centered in the middle of the screen.

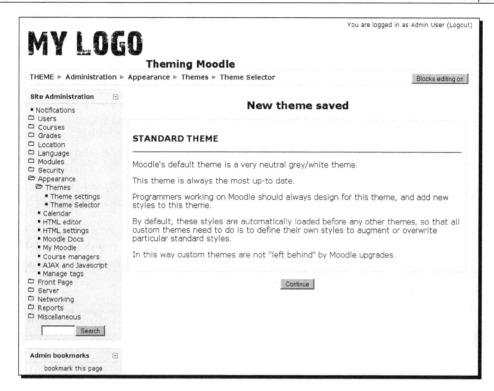

If you can't see any difference, then it is likely that the resolution on your monitor is set to 1024 x 768. Don't worry too much about this; suffice to say, if you know how to make your resolution higher, then do it, so that you can clearly see the changes that you have made. I recommend at least 1280 x 1024, but if you have a widescreen monitor or your resolution is higher, please leave it as it is.

Time for action – adding a border and some padding to your theme

Before you go through what you have learned in the last exercise, you will be making two more changes to your theme so that it stands out a little more and has slightly better padding around the edges. We will then briefly go through what we have learned in the last two exercises.

1. Open your my_style.css file and add the following lines of code to the #page class that you have already added:

```
border-style:solid;
border-color:#000000;
border-width:1px;
padding:10px;
```

So the full class now looks like this:

```
#page {
width:975px; - sets the width of the page
margin:0px auto; - overrides the default browser margins
background: #ffffff; - sets the background to white
border-style:solid; - sets the border to solid,
                          some other options are dotted and dashed
border-color:#000000; - Sets the color of the above border
                          to black
border-width:1px; - sets the width of the border to 1px
padding:10px; - sets the padding of the #page id to 10px
}
```

2. Save your `my_style.css` file and refresh your browser. Your site should look like the next screenshot. Notice the new border around the edge that makes the whole site visually stand out a little better.

You might also notice that the padding around the edge of your Moodle site has become a little bigger, that is, elements such as the *login info* link aren't positioned right up against the top border, which simply makes it look better.

What just happened?

In the first exercise, you learned how to set your Moodle site's page width using CSS. Although this isn't really recommended or practical because this reduces the space on the page for courses, you may at some point have to do this so that you can make your Moodle site match an existing corporate or institutional website. In such a case, most Moodle themers would have their Moodle front page set to a fixed width design and the courses' pages would be a full screen (liquid) design to give the users more space to work with.

In the second simple exercise, you learned how to add a border around your Moodle site and how to adjust the padding so that you have some neat whitespace around the outside. After all, there is nothing worse than a website that appears squashed.

Fixed versus liquid designs

You may have noticed that we have been discussing fixed and liquid Moodle themes in this section, and you might be wondering what exactly this means. Well, over the last ten years there has been an ongoing debate as to whether websites should be of a fixed width layout or a relative or liquid layout. This argument is likely to continue long into the future.

Fixed width designs

Fixed width designs are websites that are set to a fixed size either via the HTML or the CSS that they use and will remain this size regardless of the size of the visitor's monitor or its resolution. The exercise that you just completed turned your liquid (relative) Moodle theme into one that has a fixed width. A fixed width design doesn't have to be positioned in the middle of the screen (as ours did); it could be easily moved to the left or even to the right.

The benefits of having a fixed width design are consistency and control. The elements of a fixed width design retain their proportions regardless of the monitor's size or resolution. It's much easier for the Moodle themer to control the overall look and feel of a website by using a fixed width design.

On the downside, the designer has to decide how wide they should make their site, (for example, 1024 x 768) and stick to that resolution. So, if a visitor has a monitor size of 800 x 600, then they will have the dreaded horizontal scroll bar. Conversely, if a visitor has a very large monitor with a resolution of 1960 x 1280, then the site would be sitting in a large area of whitespace.

Liquid or relative widths

Liquid or **relative widths** use the whole of the browser window and resize to whatever size the visitor's browser window is. These designs tend to be used when the websites are information-based and contain more text than graphics. Moodle has been engineered out of the box to be a liquid design because these designs tend to have more area for content than fixed layout designs when used on larger monitors.

The benefit, as suggested, is that if the users have average to large size monitors, they tend to have more space for content. The site will expand to fit the whole screen, and therefore not waste any space.

The downside to such designs is that it's a lot harder for the designer to control the structure of the site and, in some very large monitors, the site can look rather spaced out.

What type of layout should you use?

Well, as suggested earlier, I personally believe that as Moodle is a content-based application and as it was originally engineered to have a liquid or relative layout, this is the type of design a Moodle themer should use. When it concerns normal websites that have graphical content, I prefer fixed width layout designs. But of course, Moodle wasn't designed to have one, so I would try to avoid it.

Having said that, I have had to in the past create several front page Moodle themes with fixed width layout designs so that Moodle would match the companies' corporate website. So in these terms, it is worth knowing how and when fixed width layout designs should be used.

To make this subject a little clearer, I have included some graphics here of fixed and liquid designs and the full and reduced screen variations of these.

The following design is a fixed width design with a width of 960px. This type of design will stay this size regardless of the browser window size. This is achieved by using pixels as the unit of measurement.

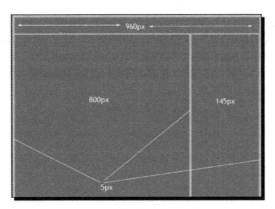

The following design is a liquid design with a width of 100%. This type of design will expand and contract as the browser window is resized. This is achieved by using percentages as the unit of measurement.

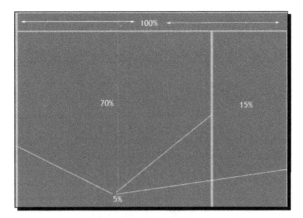

Set out next is an example as seen in the browser window. This figure shows a full screen design using the entire 1280 x 1024 browser window. Again, this technique uses percentages as its unit of measurement and therefore expands and contracts with the browser window.

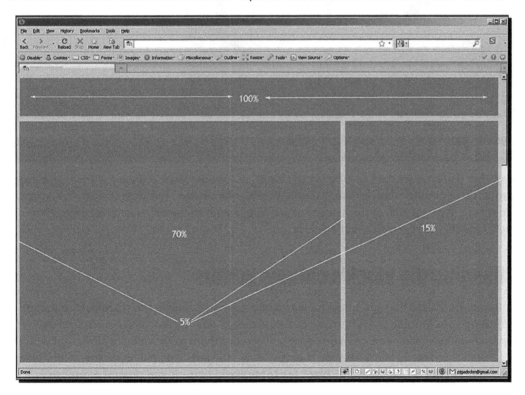

Finally, this figure shows the same size browser window using a fixed design and using pixels as its unit of measurement. Using this technique, the website remains the same size irrespective of the size to which the browser window has been set.

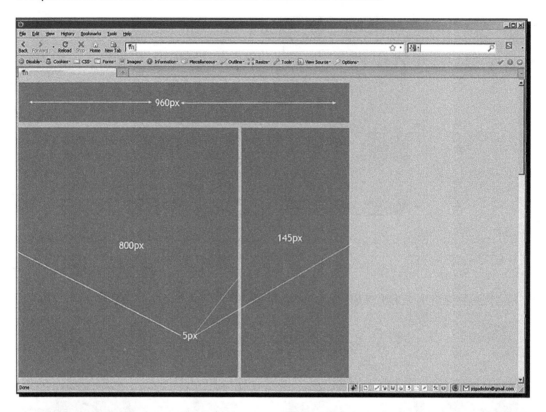

Have a go hero – set some different widths

Now that you have learned how to set the width of Moodle from a liquid (relative) to a fixed layout, try to set the width of your Moodle site to other values. For instance, you could set Moodle to use only 80% of the screen, or you could set it to use an exact pixel other than the 992px that we did in the first exercise.

Changing the block's column widths

Another layout task that you might have to undertake is to change the sideblock's column widths on your Moodle site. There are occasions when you might want the left- and the right-hand blocks thinner, or maybe you might require them to have slightly different widths. For instance, on many of my Moodle themes, I have the left-hand blocks slightly wider than the right, as I might use the HTML block for some static content and require more room.

Although the techniques required to do this are not quite the techniques used in the normal theming process (that is, not changing the CSS), they are nevertheless considered a part of Moodle theming, as they can be controlled from within our `theme` directory by using the `theme.config` file.

Time for action – changing the width of the block columns

1. Navigate to your Moodle's root folder at: `C:\Program Files\Apache Software Foundation\Apache 2.2\htdocs` and locate the `index.php` file.

2. Right-click on this file and choose **Open With | WordPad**.

3. Copy the highlighted lines of code in the following screenshot:

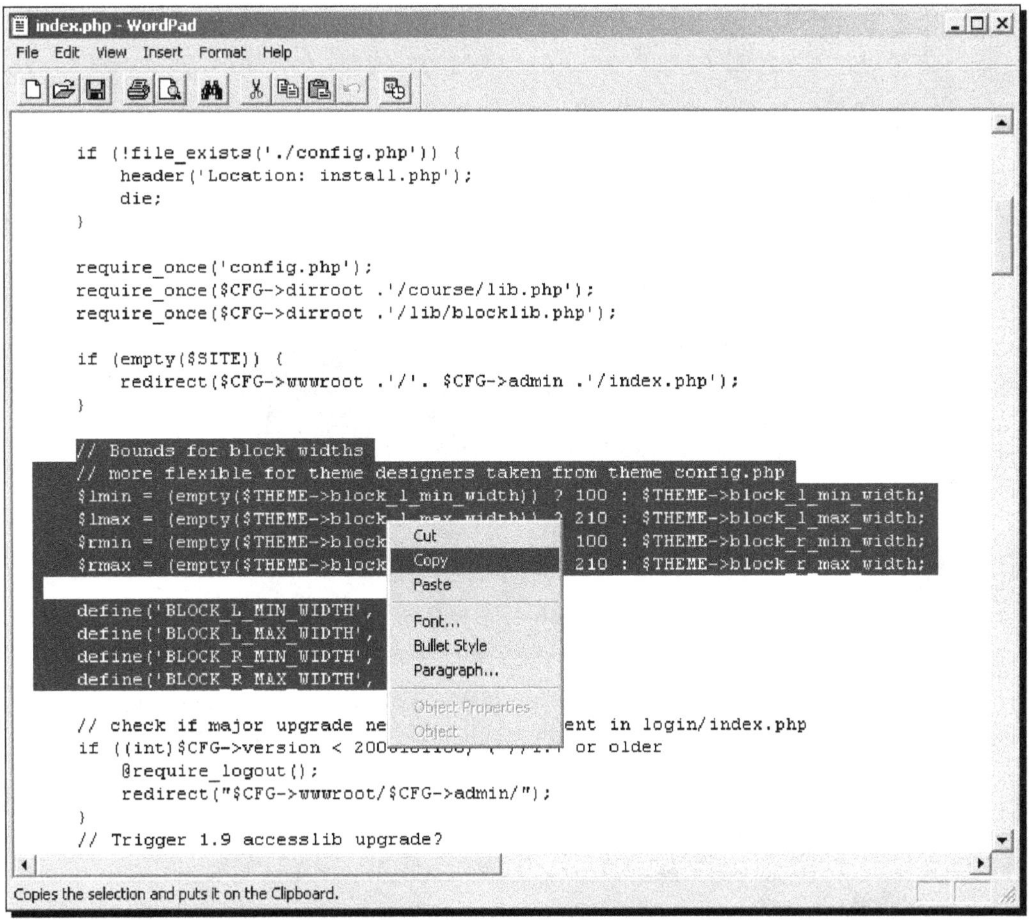

4. From **My Computer** go to `C:\Program Files\Apache Software Foundation\Apache 2.2\htdocs\Theme\mytheme` and right-click on the `config.php` file and choose **Open With | WordPad**.

5. Scroll to the bottom of the file, right-click, and choose **Paste**, as set out in the following screenshot:

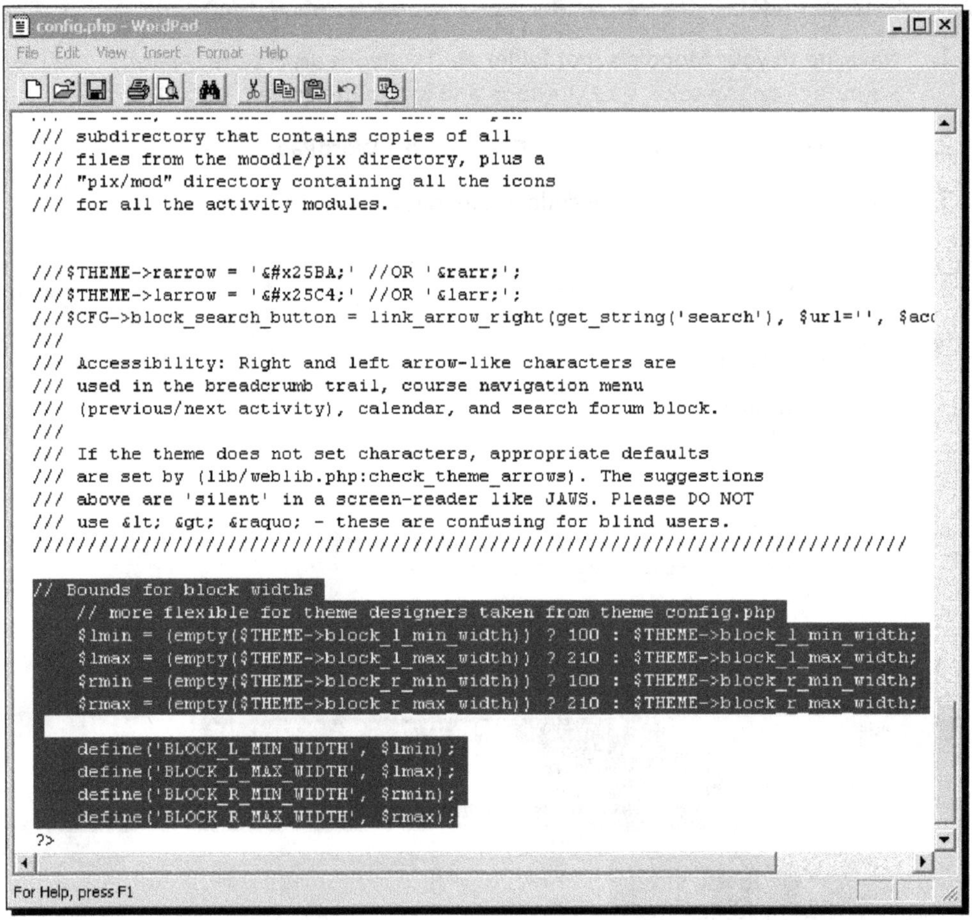

Please note that you should make sure that you place the cursor before you right-click and choose paste after the last line of forward slashes and before the last `?>`.

6. Find the following top two lines of code that you have just pasted in:

```
$lmin = (empty($THEME->block_l_min_width)) ? 100 :
$THEME->block_l_min_width;

$lmax = (empty($THEME->block_l_max_width)) ? 210 :
$THEME->block_l_max_width;
```

7. And change them to:

```
$lmin = (empty($THEME->block_l_min_width)) ? 300 :
$THEME->block_l_min_width;
$lmax = (empty($THEME->block_l_max_width)) ? 300 :
$THEME->block_l_max_width;
```

8. Save your `config` file and refresh your browser. You should notice that the administration block or any other left-hand blocks have just become wider as seen in the following screenshot:

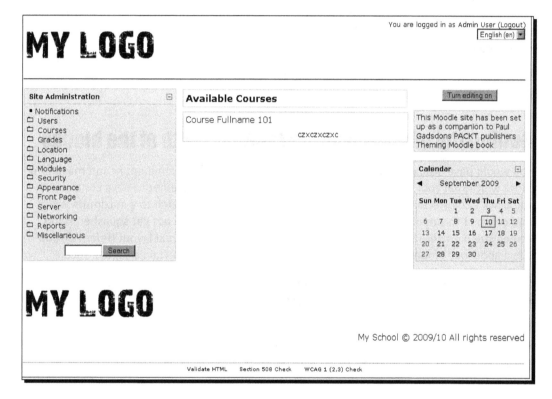

Top Tip – Changing the block widths

This technique is at present only a hack, as Moodle has various files that will override this code. I believe that there are around seven different files that might cause this technique not to work or to display erratically. If you do change the width of the blocks, then I would recommend that you test the outcome not only in different browsers but also in different areas of your Moodle application. There may be modules and/or resources that will override your code. This bug has been logged with `Moodle.org`.

What just happened?

In the last exercise, you learned that block widths are controlled by a section of code in the `index.php` file, which is located in the root of your Moodle site. You have also learned that by moving this to your `mytheme` folder's `config.php` file (not the other `config.php` file in Moodle's root) in the root of your `mytheme` folder, you can override any (most of) Moodle blocks' left and right column width code. Finally, you have learned that you only need to make some small changes to the block of code in order to change the default block widths.

It's worth noting at this stage that if you use a fixed width layout for your Moodle theme, this technique makes less of an impact because you have a smaller area to work with. Therefore, changing the block widths would not ordinarily be done in a fixed width layout unless you only need to make the blocks thinner rather than wider.

Thus in this context, it would be appropriate for you to go back and change the block widths back to their original sizes for now.

Setting the minimum and maximum width of the blocks

You would have noticed in the last couple of tasks that there was a minimum and maximum block width that could be set. This setting enables the Moodle themer to have control over the block's column widths in such a way that the columns will stretch to a maximum width and contract to a minimum width, so that the block's contents do not get squashed if the screen size is small. This will work only if you have a full-screen liquid layout (relative), and it is a good way of making sure that your blocks remain within a certain size tolerance.

In the last exercise, you set both the minimum and the maximum block sizes to the same values because you currently have a fixed width layout.

In the next exercise, you will be setting both the minimum and the maximum block widths to different values. In order to see this work properly, you will have to change your theme from a fixed width layout back to the original liquid layout.

Time for action – changing our theme back to a liquid layout

1. Navigate to `C:\Program Files\Apache Software Foundation\Apache 2.2\htdocs\theme\mytheme` and open your `my_style.css` file using WordPad as we have learned in the previous exercises.

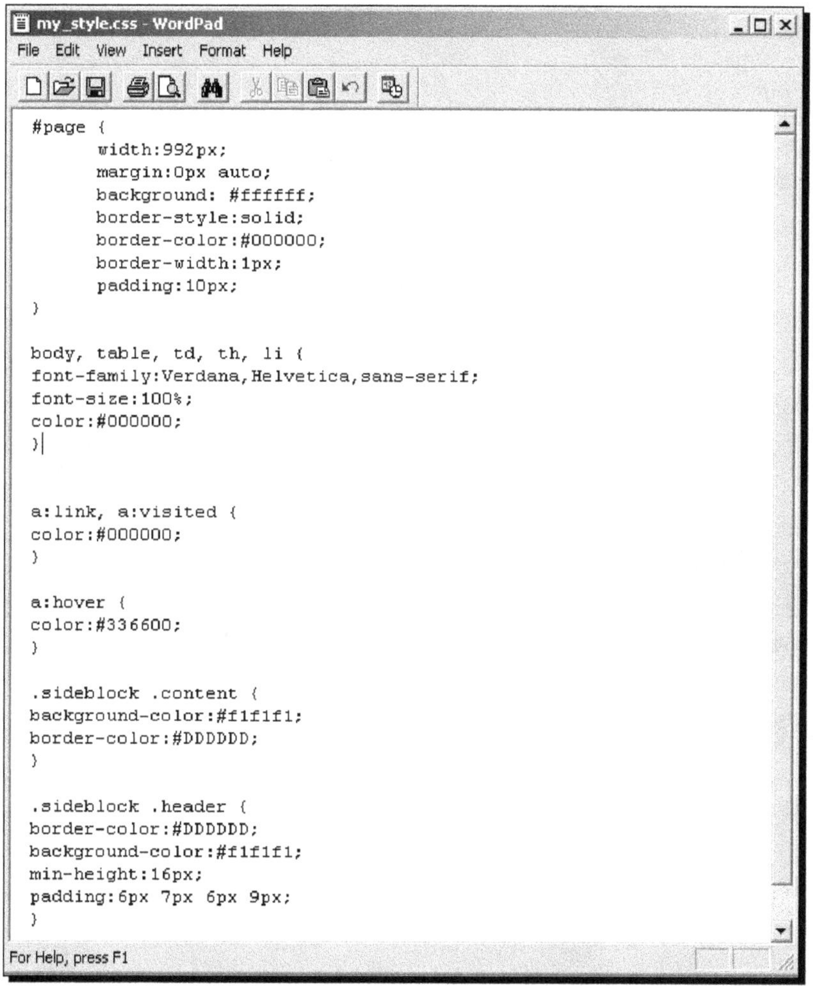

my_style.css - WordPad
File Edit View Insert Format Help
#page {
width:992px;
margin:0px auto;
background: #ffffff;
border-style:solid;
border-color:#000000;
border-width:1px;
padding:10px;
}
body, table, td, th, li {
font-family:Verdana,Helvetica,sans-serif;
font-size:100%;
color:#000000;
}
a:link, a:visited {
color:#000000;
}
a:hover {
color:#336600;
}
.sideblock .content {
background-color:#f1f1f1;
border-color:#DDDDDD;
}
.sideblock .header {
border-color:#DDDDDD;
background-color:#f1f1f1;
min-height:16px;
padding:6px 7px 6px 9px;
}
For Help, press F1

2. Remove the whole `#page` selector and save your `my_style.css` file.

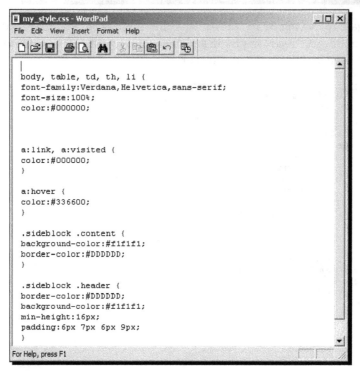

3. Refresh your browser by pressing the *F5* key. You will notice that your Moodle site now fills the whole browser screen as seen below:

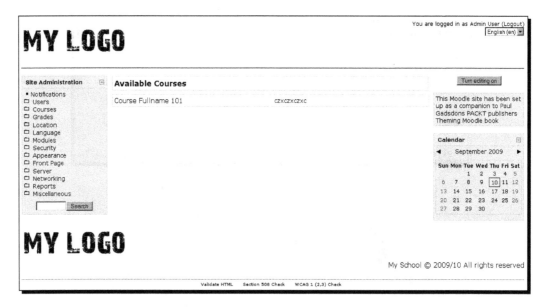

4. Press the **Restore Down** button on your browser, which is located at the top right-hand corner and is displayed below. Your browser should become smaller, and this will enable you to drag it to make it smaller or larger.

5. Click on the corner of your browser and resize it by grabbing the top-right corner and dragging it in and out to make the window smaller and bigger. Notice how your Moodle site stretches and contracts (liquid), and if you make it really small, the administration block shrinks to the minimum that you allowed in your block's width code in the `config.php` file of `mytheme`. At first, your screen may look like the following screenshot:

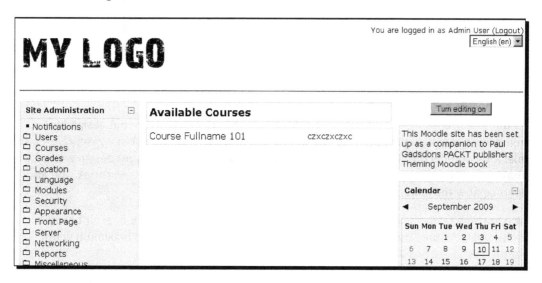

The following screenshot is the same screen as the previous one, except that it has been reduced in size to show its resized liquid (relative) design itself.

What just happened?

In this exercise, you simply changed your Moodle site back to a liquid layout design by removing the #page class that you had added in a previous task from your my_style.css file. After you did this, you looked in more detail into how the liquid layout design works by making your browser window larger and smaller to see the site stretch and shrink. You also learned how the minimum block width setting works.

You are now ready to change the minimum block width setting so that it doesn't become quite small. Assume that you need your left-hand blocks' minimum and maximum width settings as 150px and 250px.

Time for action – setting the minimum and maximum block widths

1. From **My Computer** go to C:\Program Files\Apache Software Foundation\Apache 2.2\htdocs\theme\mytheme and right-click on the config.php file and choose **Open With | WordPad**.

2. Scroll to the bottom of the file and find the block width section of code.

Point to note:

You may have noticed that although the right-hand block's minimum width setting is the same as the left-hand one, it didn't get any smaller. This is because the calendar is one of the blocks that has its own block width settings and this is covered by the issues with block widths that you learned about in an earlier section.

So, the only way to test the right-hand minimum width setting is to delete the calendar block. This can be added back at any time.

This is a Moodle bug and has been reported as such.

```
config.php - WordPad                                        _□×
File  Edit  View  Insert  Format  Help

 D 🖆 🔲 🎒 🔍 🛤 ✂ 📋 📋 ↻ 📑

/// subdirectory that contains copies of all
/// files from the moodle/pix directory, plus a
/// "pix/mod" directory containing all the icons
/// for all the activity modules.


///$THEME->rarrow = '&#x25BA;' //OR '&rarr;';
///$THEME->larrow = '&#x25C4;' //OR '&larr;';
///$CFG->block_search_button = link_arrow_right(get_string('search'), $url='', $acc
///
/// Accessibility: Right and left arrow-like characters are
/// used in the breadcrumb trail, course navigation menu
/// (previous/next activity), calendar, and search forum block.
///
/// If the theme does not set characters, appropriate defaults
/// are set by (lib/weblib.php:check_theme_arrows). The suggestions
/// above are 'silent' in a screen-reader like JAWS. Please DO NOT
/// use &lt; &gt; &raquo; - these are confusing for blind users.
////////////////////////////////////////////////////////////////

// Bounds for block widths
    // more flexible for theme designers taken from theme config.php
    $lmin = (empty($THEME->block_l_min_width)) ? 100 : $THEME->block_l_min_width;
    $lmax = (empty($THEME->block_l_max_width)) ? 210 : $THEME->block_l_max_width;
    $rmin = (empty($THEME->block_r_min_width)) ? 100 : $THEME->block_r_min_width;
    $rmax = (empty($THEME->block_r_max_width)) ? 210 : $THEME->block_r_max_width;


    define('BLOCK_L_MIN_WIDTH', $lmin);
    define('BLOCK_L_MAX_WIDTH', $lmax);
    define('BLOCK_R_MIN_WIDTH', $rmin);
    define('BLOCK_R_MAX_WIDTH', $rmax);
?>

For Help, press F1
```

3. Find the following top two lines of code in the block width code section:

```
$lmin = (empty($THEME->block_l_min_width)) ? 100 :
$THEME->block_l_min_width;

$lmax = (empty($THEME->block_l_max_width)) ? 210 :
$THEME->block_l_max_width;
```

4. And change them to:

```
$lmin = (empty($THEME->block_l_min_width)) ? 150 :
$THEME->block_l_min_width;

$lmax = (empty($THEME->block_l_max_width)) ? 250 :
$THEME->block_l_max_width;
```

5. Save your `config` file and refresh your browser.

6. Now **Restore Down** your browser window by grabbing the corner as you did in the previous task, and make the window small again. You should see that the left-hand administration block does not become so small anymore. You would also notice that when the window is made larger, the block will grow to a maximum of 250px.

What just happened?

In this simple exercise, you continued from the previous task and learned how the minimum and maximum block width settings affect how Moodle resizes in a liquid layout. You should now understand that you can set these parameters to ensure that your site displays correctly in any screen size.

Have a go hero – change your sideblocks again

By using what you have learned so far, go back and change your sideblocks such that the left-hand blocks have a minimum of 200px and a maximum of 300px. Do this for the right-hand blocks also, but let them have a slightly thinner maximum size of 250px.

Pop quiz

Q1. What layout type is recommended for use with Moodle?

    A. Liquid (relative)

    B. Fixed

Q2. Where does one set the minimum and maximum column widths for blocks?

    A. `htdocs\theme\my_theme\config.php`

    B. `htdocs\theme\config.php`

Q3. Why should we take care when we change the block width code?

    A. Because Moodle has to have a certain block width

    B. Because Moodle has a bug, which means that some blocks and resources have this setting hardcoded

    C. Block widths have an effect on the course layout

Summary

In this chapter, you have covered the differences between fixed and liquid themes and what you need to do in order to change your theme's layout. You have also learned how to change the widths of the sideblocks and should now understand the minimum and maximum settings for these.

Specifically, we covered:

- What the differences are between fixed and liquid Moodle themes
- How easy it is to set the theme's width using CSS and why you might need to do this
- How to change the sideblock widths

Now that you've learned about changing Moodle's layouts, let's move on to the second part of this book, where you will start to learn how to create your own theme from scratch. The first chapter in part two will be focusing on the planning stage of creating a Moodle theme.

6
Planning your Moodle Theme

Chapter 6 will introduce the concept of "know your audience" and expand on this by making sure that you create your own goals for your Moodle theme before moving on to the "planning and gathering assets" stage. In this section, you will learn about the need to think about the images or graphics that might be required, and will also learn to decide whether animation or static graphics should be used—depending on the audience. Informal research will be the key to this stage. We will then address how we should create the design for the Moodle theme—from a simple paper mockup to a full blown exact copy by using graphics software (a scamp).

In this chapter, we shall cover:

◆ Knowing our audience

◆ Gathering our assets

◆ Designing our theme

◆ Creating a mockup using software

So let's crack on...

Important preliminary points

For this chapter, we will be discussing the different methods that you can use to create a design on which to base your Moodle theme. We will also introduce graphics software packages such as Adobe Photoshop, Adobe Photoshop Elements, and Gimp (which is an open source equivalent to Adobe Photoshop). Because this book isn't about learning how to use Adobe Photoshop, it is assumed that you have some graphic design experience, and that Photoshop can easily be supplanted by any graphic manipulation software package, preferably the one that you know how to use.

Know your audience

One of the key tasks that any Moodle themer needs to understand is the importance of knowing their audience. This is the case with any type of design and development work—that is, key to creating a theme that fits the identified target audience.

Design wise

One of the first things that you need to decide, long before you put pen to paper, is who your audience is and with whom you are trying to communicate.

So who are the people who will be using your Moodle application? This is a far more important question than it appears on the surface, as it will define and guide you through the initial stages of implementing a new theme for your Moodle site. It is very important to understand that you will not be able to design a theme for Moodle that will communicate the intentions of a Moodle learning environment to everyone. Different groups of users will require different approaches to theme design. For example, if your Moodle site is aimed at the under-12 age group, then visually it will be very different from a Moodle site that is aimed at a corporate environment.

So let's sit back for a minute or two and think carefully about what your audience will require from your planned Moodle theme.

We are obviously going to create a Moodle theme with education in mind, but what level of education? Will your organization be using Moodle as a corporate training tool? Are you in higher education and will the Moodle site be aimed at degree-level students? Or is Moodle being set up to educate children?

All of these factors will influence not only how Moodle looks but also how people interact with it.

Technology wise

As you have discovered in the previous chapters, differing technologies can cause issues with the Moodle theming process, and as such this is an important factor when it comes to knowing your audience. You have discovered that screen resolution, screen size, and computer platforms all have an impact on how you design Moodle themes. For instance, if you are designing a Moodle theme that will be used in a corporate environment as a training tool, it is likely to be run on an intranet. This means that only internal staff would be able to gain access, and therefore you might not need to accommodate so many different platform variables such as browser type, screen size, and so on. These are often set by the organization's IT department, so most users will be using the same platform, browser type, and screen size.

However, if the Moodle site is going to be used internally and externally (as in the case of higher education students), then you have no control over what browser they use and what screen size they have. Of course, it is always best to create Moodle themes that work on all platforms and browsers. However, this is not always possible given budget or time constraints. After all, there will always be one or two people who will be using Opera 2.3 on Red Hat Linux! However, if you do have any issues while designing Moodle themes, these can normally be resolved with a little patience from yourself and maybe some help from the Moodle community.

Again, if you are using Moodle in a large educational or commercial environment, then it is worth asking your ITC department for some statistics on browser type, platform, and resolution. Most organizations will have this information from web statistics programs, such as Webalizer, AWStats, or maybe Google Analytics. You can then decide on the lowest common denominator and choose what browsers and screen sizes to support, and what others are considered defunct or legacy. But given this advice it is always best to try to be the best themer, by providing a working solution for as many users as possible.

Some questions before you begin

In order to plan an effective theme implementation for your organization, there will be some questions that you will need to find answers for. To help in this process, some of the more obvious ones are set out here:

- Who is your primary audience? Are they children, young adults in higher education, or employees in the public or private sector?
- Can you make assumptions by gathering statistical information about an average user's connection speed, browser type, resolution, and screen size? You need to make the most of our resources here.
- What resources do you have? Time, staff, money, and so forth.
- Is your Moodle site a part of a larger group of Moodle sites, or does your organization have a defined brand? If so, do you need to provide the same look and feel?

Theming for education

So you have three different groups represented in general education (primary, secondary, and higher education), and although they are different educational groups, they can really be split into age groups. The higher education group, for instance, would require a different approach to theming from pre-school age groups insofar as your design would have to be more visually appealing for the latter educational group. They will typically not want a corporate design and would require a more friendly, social, and academic look and feel. What constitutes an academic design? Well, that would probably need some research into what design elements this age and educational group would require. Also, as higher education will have a proportion of more mature learners, you should also consider that this age group might have visual or physical difficulties that will require a different theming approach again. Most countries now have laws in place to ensure that websites can be accessed by everyone. We shall discuss this a little later.

High schoolers, on the other hand, would probably require a slightly different look and feel than higher education. Fonts and colors would probably change and the design would have to be more fun to look at than a Moodle site built for a university.

Younger children between 6 and 11 years of age would again require a different approach. A Moodle site aimed at this age group would require bright colors and fun graphics. A Moodle site with no graphics and just basic corporate fonts would not appeal to this audience. There are a couple of themes available on `Moodle.org` that are squarely aimed at different age groups. Have a look at some of these now, as this will help you to decide what you might require in terms of your Moodle theme.

Time for action – downloading and installing a theme for children

1. Open your web browser and navigate to `http://moodle.org/mod/data/view.php?d=26&rid=1958`, or alternatively just go to `http://moodle.org` and click on **Downloads | Themes** and then find the *Children Education* theme.

2. Click on the **Download** link, which will take you to the website of this template's author.

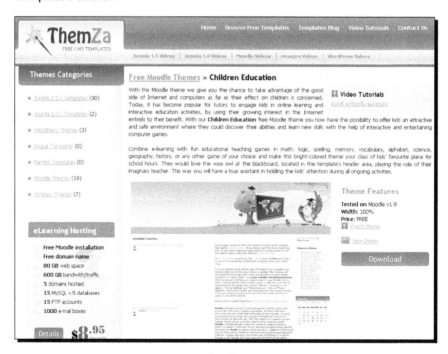

3. Click the large **Download** button on the right-hand side and download this theme to your desktop.

4. Right-click on the downloaded `children-education.zip` file and choose **ZipGenius | Extract Here**.

5. Copy the extracted `children-education` folder by right-clicking on it and choosing **Copy**.

6. Navigate to `C:\Program Files\Apache Software Foundation\Apache 2.2\htdocs\theme`.

7. Paste your new theme in this folder by right-clicking on the folder and choosing **Paste**.

8. Open your Moodle site in another browser window or tab, and navigate to: **Site Administration | Appearance | Themes | Theme Selector**. Scroll down until you see your new *Children Education* theme. Click on the theme to select it, and then click on the **Choose** button.

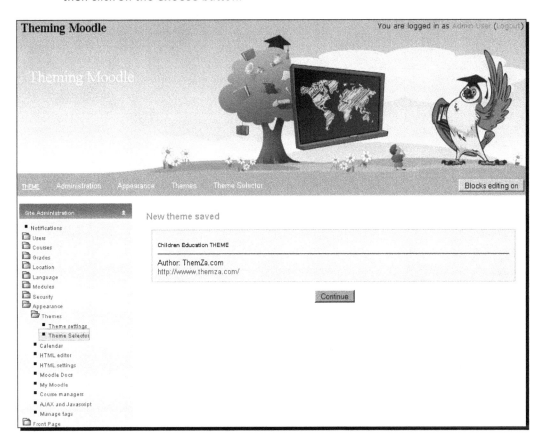

As you can see, this theme is firmly aimed at a younger audience—it has bright colors and fun graphics placed in the header. Now download and install some themes more suitable for those above 12 years and for users in higher education. As you have downloaded quite a few themes now, it won't be necessary to go through the process step-by-step. You should now know how to do it by now.

Time for action – downloading and installing themes for those above 12 years old

1. Navigate to `Moodle.org`.

2. Download the *Clouds* theme.

3. Install this theme.

4. Using the **Theme Selector**, choose this theme.

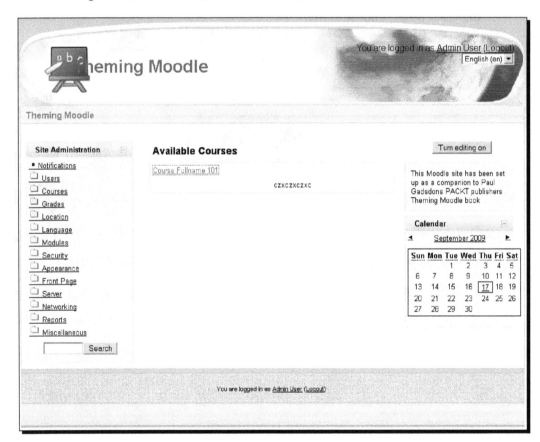

This theme again is aimed at children but is primarily aimed at those above 12 years of age—it has slightly less bright colors and less colorful graphics. Make up your mind here because this is down to what you feel would be appropriate given your situation. Suffice it to say that these are only examples designed to get you thinking about what you might require from your own Moodle themes.

Finally, have a look at a theme that is aimed squarely at the higher education sector and compare the three themes that you have. There will be some very obvious differences, but also some subtle differences that you might not have noticed.

Time for action – downloading a Moodle theme for higher education

1. Browse to `Moodle.org`.

2. Go to the **Themes** section and download the *Student Experience* theme.

3. Install this theme and change your Moodle site to use this theme.

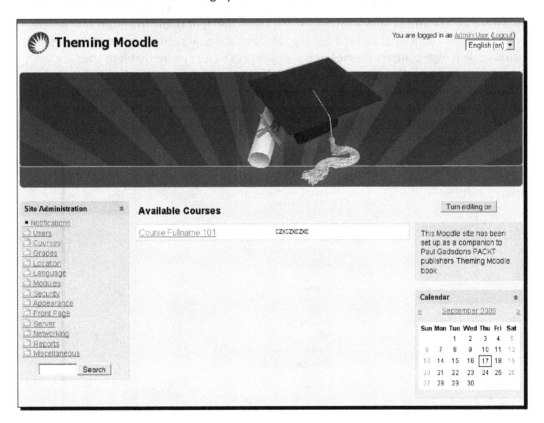

As you can see, this theme is aimed at the higher education sector and is therefore clean and simple. It has graphics that are associated with the higher education sector, accompanied by nice, clean, and simple fonts.

What just happened?

You have just downloaded a theme from `Moodle.org` that has been specifically designed for children. This should give you some idea on what you might need to consider when theming for children. You have also learned that `Moodle.org` isn't the only site where you can find free open source Moodle themes.

Theming for disabilities

You must always try to ensure that your Moodle themes meet the recommended accessibility guidelines of the country that the Moodle site is aimed at. However, there might also be a specific requirement to ensure that people with physical and/or mental disabilities can still gain access to and use your Moodle site. Although most of these issues are aimed at Moodle as an application, there are still things that you can do as a Moodle themer to make access for people with disabilities easier. You could, for instance, create a Moodle theme that has a good contrast between background colors and font colors to ensure that people who have visual difficulties can still see the words on the pages. These types of themes are usually called **high-contrast themes** or designs. You can also ensure that font sizes are set as percentages in the theme's CSS file so that the users can increase the font size in their browsers. The following screenshot is an example of a high-contrast theme that can also be customized and used by people with various visual disabilities. For these reasons, it is preferred that people should be able to choose their own themes in Moodle, rather than being forced to.

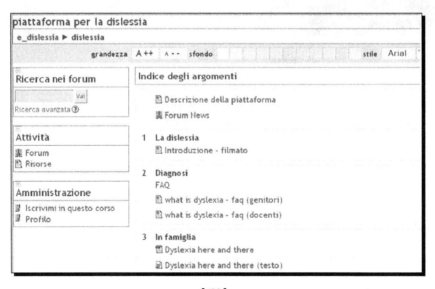

Gathering our assets

In this stage of the development process, you need to think about getting all of your assets together before you create your first proper Moodle theme. **Assets** are all of the different elements that you will need to use in order for you to complete your Moodle theme. These can include institutional logos, color schemes, graphics, font types, icons, and even text content for the header and footer sections of your planned Moodle theme.

It is very important to think about this at this stage and to ensure that all of the branding requirements of the institution have been met, as there is nothing worse than creating a great theme only to be told that you have used the wrong color scheme or font. So networking is the game here! You must make sure that you find out exactly what is required in terms of branding at this stage. I often find that the first ports of call on this subject are often the web developers/designers and/or the marketing department.

Another reason why you would need to "*gather your assets*" is to ensure that the development stage of creating your Moodle theme isn't broken up too much by having to source logos, text, or color schemes. This process can often take quite a while and could therefore create delays in the building of your Moodle theme if done later in the development phase.

Some more questions to ask

If you gather your assets in the right way and ask the right questions as you start to plan your Moodle theme, then delays can be avoided. The following questions can be used to make sure that you get the organization's brand correct before you start developing your theme:

- Does your organization have a specific font or font size that you need to use?
- Does it have a specific color scheme?
- What is your Moodle site going to be called? (This will have an impact on the logo and/or title.)
- Is there a branding message (strapline) that needs to be used?
- Do you need specific icons in your theme?

The pix folder

We briefly mentioned the `pix` folder in *Chapter 2, Moodle Themes*. This folder is the main image folder for a Moodle theme and contains all of the images, such as tabs and all of the icons, used throughout in a theme. If you or the organization that you work for decides that you need a custom set of icons for your Moodle theme, then this will also have an impact on the asset-gathering stage of your project.

The icons used in your Moodle site are located in the `\htdocs\pix` folder. These are the standard default icons that can be used if you do not wish to use your own custom icons for your theme. Custom theme-specific icons will be stored in the `\htdocs\theme\[your chosen theme]` directory and will load depending on the Moodle theme's `config.php` file's settings.

Therefore, the Moodle application will look at the theme's `config.php` file first. If the `custom pix` setting is set to `True`, Moodle will use the `pix` folder in your chosen theme's folder.

This is very useful, as you might only want to change the course icons for your theme. In this case, you can just copy the `C` folder from `Moodle\pix` and paste it into the `Moodle\htdocs\[your theme]\pix` folder and overwrite these. You can then replace the icons in this folder with the ones that you prefer.

The subdirectories inside the `\pix` folder organize the icons based on their specific purpose in the Moodle application. Set out below are the usual icon folders and their corresponding uses:

- **a**: Navigation icons used for the breadcrumb navigation elements.
- **c**: Contains the icons related to Moodle courses.
- **f**: Contains icons for the different file formats handled by Moodle, such as Word and PDF.
- **g**: Contains the teacher profile images. There are two default images in here—one large and one small smiley face.
- **i**: Contains navigation and function icons, such as the *edit*, *hide*, and *show* icons.
- **m**: Contains the different currency icons.
- **s**: Contains the smileys for smile, wink, and sad.
- **t**: Contains the icons for the teacher functions, such as backup, restore, delete, and hide.
- **u**: Contains the images used with student profiles; this folder has two default images—one large and one small.

Any of these icons can be replaced, either one at a time or all in one go. In Chapter 8, we will learn how to do this. Suffice it to say that for now all you need to do is decide if you will be using any custom icons, and then gather these assets for the next couple of chapters.

Designing your design

After you have done all of the research necessary to make sure that you have all of the assets in place to create your Moodle theme, you will need to plan a design. The first stage in this process is to browse through the Internet for designs that you like, and see if you can replicate them in Moodle. I don't mean make an exact copy of a website that you might see, as Moodle has specific elements that need to be considered, such as the sideblocks, the administration screens, and so on. However, you can copy a color scheme, or the structure of a website, such as its navigation structure, its menu, or header layout. If you have a closer look at Moodle, it is relatively easy to see what elements can be copied from other websites or from other Moodle themes.

So let's go and have a look at some other Moodle sites.

Time for action – looking at other Moodle sites

1. Open your web browser and navigate to `http://moodle.org/sites/`.

2. Roll your mouse over the **Community** link and choose **Registered sites** from the drop-down menu.

3. Click on the country that you wish to see the other Moodle sites from (I have chosen USA).

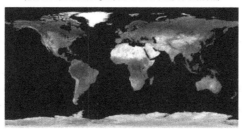

4. If you scroll down the page, you will see a long list of Moodle sites that are hosted in the selected country (USA in my example).

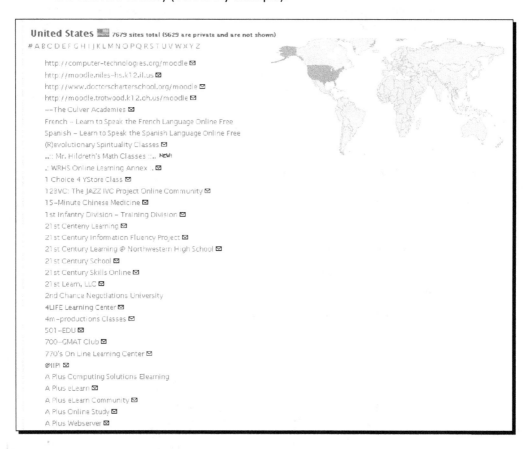

You now need to have a really close look at as many of these sites as you can, so that you can get an idea of what you might want from your planned Moodle theme. It is definitely worth taking notes at this stage, otherwise you might forget some of the elements that you would like as apart of your own theme. Don't take hours and hours here because you will very quickly go beyond the point that this exercise becomes useful. It is also worth pointing out that not all of the sites listed will allow us access. If so, just go to another one. It is also worth noting that the sites that have a little smiley face next to them have been voted as good.

Creating our design on paper

Now that you have had a good look at some other Moodle sites, you should have a better idea of how your Moodle theme could look, or at least have an idea of the fonts and colors that you might want to use. With this in mind you now need to move on to the actual designing stage of creating your Moodle theme. I normally find it useful to grab a sheet of paper at this stage and simply draw a basic design of the theme that I intend to build. I don't mean an exact artist's impression here—only a rough structural layout of where the main elements are, and what the headers and footers should look like. But remember that Moodle does have a rather restrictive layout anyway, so you need to have left- and right-hand blocks and a header and footer. I can't draw these for you, so I will give you an example to show you how this works.

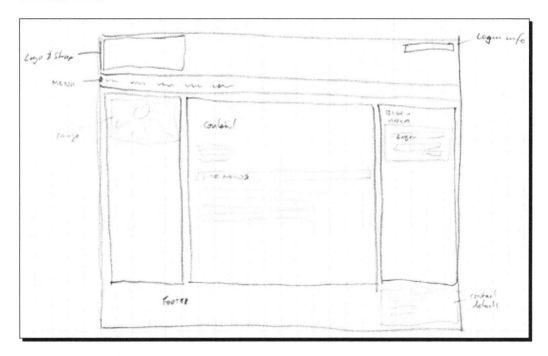

As you can see, this is just a basic sketch of what you think you want, with some notes written down the side. These notes can include information such as colors, font types, logo sizes, and background colors.

Creating a wireframe

A **wireframe** is simply a graphic or sketch of the main areas, minus any text or detail, of the page that you are planning. It is similar to the first paper sketch but would contain no details at all. Planning out a wireframe also helps develop a hierarchy and gives an insight into the best positions for key elements of the theme. But remember that Moodle has a specific way of rendering blocks, headers and footers, and so on. So there are certain restrictions as to what you can and can't do.

Once you have a wireframe and a simple sketch of your thoughts, you can use these not only to help you visualize your final design but also to gauge what other people (stakeholders) in your organization feel about the concept.

Assume that after some consultation you have decided that the basic structure of your Moodle theme is going to look like the wireframe in the preceding figure. You now need to create a full graphic of your site so that you can fully visualize exactly what it is going to look like. This step is not always necessary, but it will save a lot of time in the long run. If your boss asks you to make a few changes to the final design, it's much easier to use a graphic than to go back and change the CSS or HTML. I have been using this technique for many years and insist that the final design is signed off before I do any coding or theming at all.

Creating a mockup using software

If you do not want to create your theme's design outline on paper, then there are tools available to help your create and visualize theme designs. One particular package called **Balsamiq Mockups** seems to be at the forefront of this technology, and I am reliably informed that Moodle.org uses this software package to help visualize designs and the flow of information through Moodle applications.

The following figure depicts a Balsamiq web application:

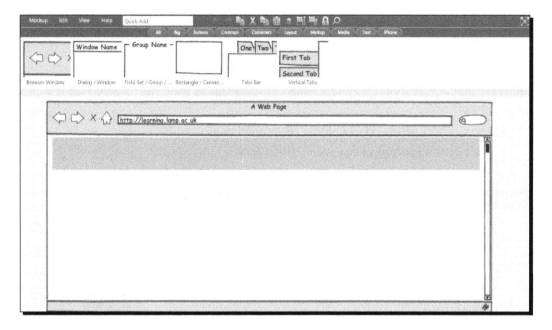

Here is a figure of our wireframe made by using Balsamiq Mockups but in more detail. As you can see, it's very easy to conceptualize the design and even the general Moodle functionality by using such software.

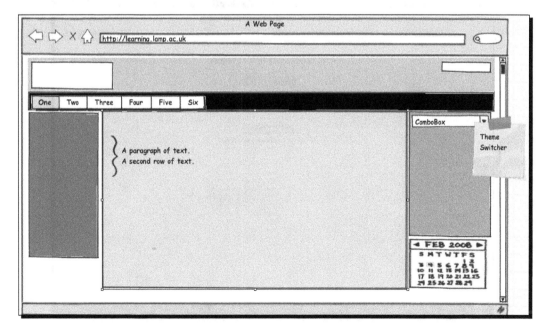

This software is not free and is priced at $79. So if you are creating only one theme for Moodle, it might be a cost too far. However, at $79, it's not a huge expense for a commercial organization. You can try it for free by using the web-based version. Go and have a look; I think you will find it rather refreshing:

Balsamiq Mockups—`http://www.balsamiq.com/`

There are many other mockup software packages available as well. The following list is a small example:

- `http://iplotz.com`—Another really good one!
- `http://mockupscreens.com`—Good again!

Creating a design using graphics software

If you look closely at the following design, you will notice that all of the details of the header are clearly marked out from the previous wireframe example. All I have done here is taken the wireframe and filled it with the most common elements that belong to all Moodle themes. I have then filled in the block areas with the colors that I want to use, and finally I made the left and right sideblocks a little prettier. For now, the most important area is the header, as this is what you will be concentrating on first.

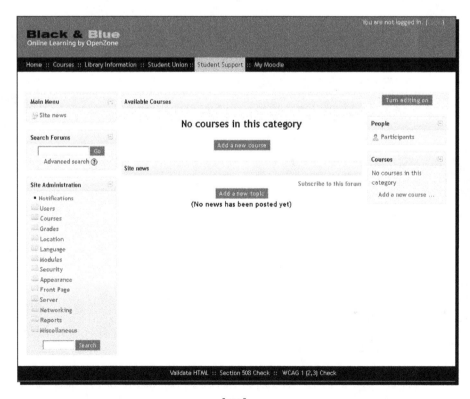

This .psd file can be downloaded from the Packt website if needed.

It's basic but functional and doesn't require too much Photoshop manipulation. In actual fact, the only parts that really need Photoshop are the logo and block headers, but for the sake of having something to compare against while you create your own theme, it would be best if you build this design in Photoshop beforehand. If you do not have Photoshop, then any other graphics manipulation software package will do as long as you are familiar with it.

Time for action – creating the header, footer, and menu in Photoshop

1. Open Photoshop (or any other image manipulation package), go to **File | New**, and create a new document with the following settings:

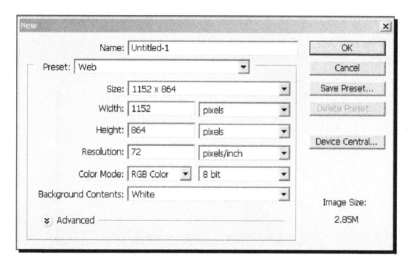

I prefer to use a widescreen resolution, as it frames the theme nicely and gives an indication about how people will view your theme on wider monitors.

2. Make sure that you have the **Info** window open by going to the menu bar and then clicking on **Window | Info**.

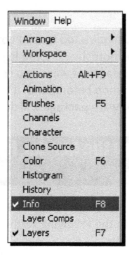

The **Info** palette will appear on your left-hand side palettes menu, and will allow you to measure areas within Photoshop.

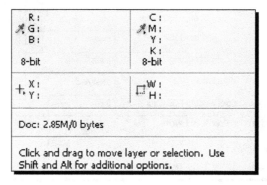

3. Click on the **Rectangular Marquee** tool.

4. Draw a rectangle selection across the whole document. Make this 90px high. You can see its height, as you make the rectangle selection, in the **Info** palette.

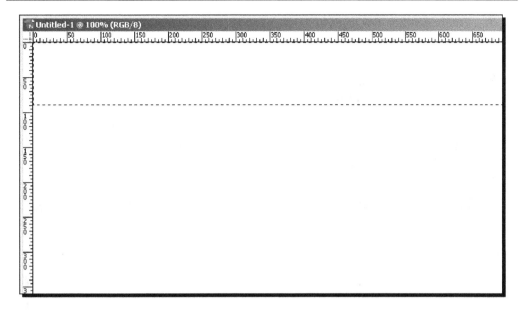

5. Go to the color chooser and click on **foreground color**, and choose the color that you want and then click **OK**.

6. Choose **File | Layer | New**.

7. Choose **File | Edit File | Fill and then Select | Deselect**.

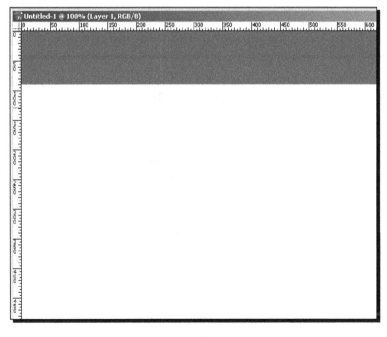

8. Create another new layer, and using your rectangular marquee make a selection across the document, just below the other layer that you first created. Make this selection 31px in height.

9. Change the foreground color from blue to black, and then choose **File | Edit | Fill**. Then choose **Select | Deselect**.

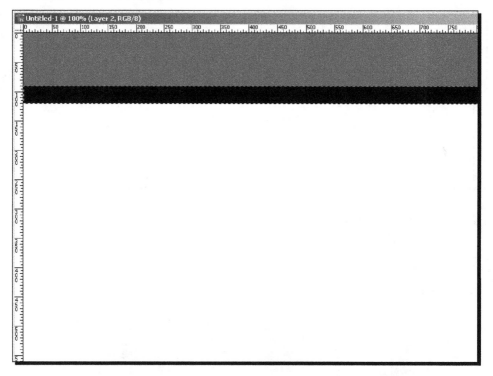

10. Go to the layers palette and right-click on the layer that you have just created, and then choose **Duplicate Layer**; then click on **OK**.

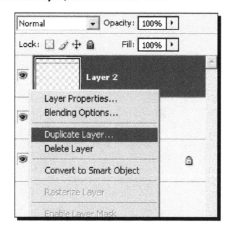

11. Click on the **Move** tool on the tools palette, and drag your newly created layer (the black strip) about three quarters of the way down the page.

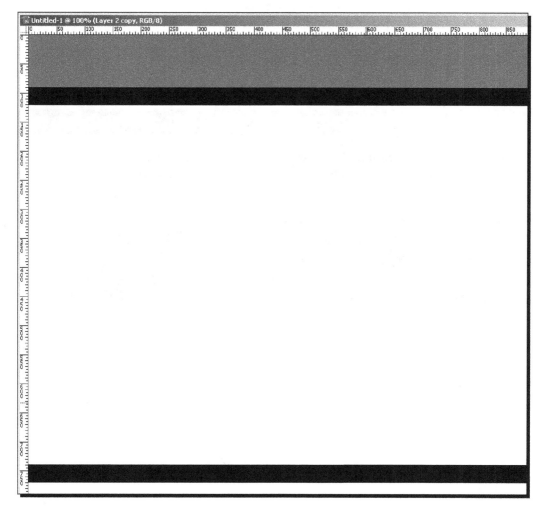

What just happened?

You have created the basic header, footer, and menu structure in Photoshop as a reference so that later you can start to edit the CSS of your theme and build your design. You have also learned some basic Photoshop skills that will help you with the upcoming tasks.

In the next task, you will create your logo and menu text, and finish off by creating the login info text. I have used a font called *Swiss 721 blkEx Bt* for the main logo text and *Frutiger 55 Roman* for the strapline, because they are nice and clean. However, you may not have these fonts, so just choose any font that is nice, clean, and heavy so that the main logo text stands out. Something such as *Impact* would do for the main logo. Alternatively, you could search on Google for **Free Swiss font download** and **Free Frutiger 55 Roman download**. A couple of good free font websites are:

- `http://www.1001freefonts.com/`
- `http://www.dafont.com/`

Time for action – creating the logo, menu text, and login info text

1. Select the text tool and click on the blue header, and then type in the words **Black & Blue**. Press the *Enter/Return* key, and then type the words **Online learning by Openzone**.

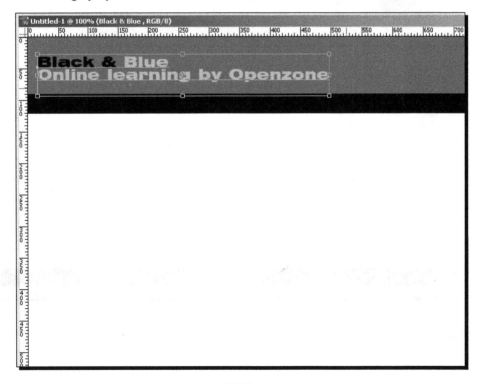

2. Using your text tool, highlight the top line of text and choose a suitable font from the text menu below the file menu, and set the same colors as set out in the preceding screenshot. The colors are #000000 and #a1b2f0.

3. Now highlight the bottom line of text and do the same, but choose the following settings. Substitute the font for something thinner if you don't have the *Frutiger* font.

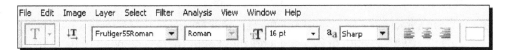

4. Click on the text tool again and click on the top black menu bar that you created earlier and type out the following text:

5. Highlight this text with the text tool and use the following settings to position the text correctly:

6. Use the text tool again and click on the large blue header on the left-hand side and enter the following text: **You are not logged in**. Don't worry too much about its positioning.

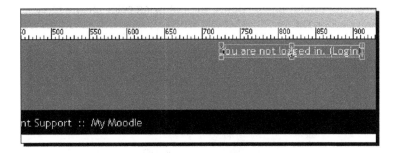

What just happened?

You have added your logo to the header section in your Photoshop file, and have also added some text elements, such as the menu text links and the login link. It is worth noting that the text links can be anything that you can link to from within Moodle, and therefore you might have a different idea as to what you want on the menu bar.

The next exercise will be slightly harder insofar as you now have to make a block in Photoshop and subsequently use gradients and rounded corners. You need to create only one block here, as all of the other blocks will use the same colors and background. I have included more than one block in my finished design scamp only so that you could get an idea of the look of the finished site.

Time for action – creating a block graphic by using Photoshop

1. Create a new layer and select the **Rectangular Marquee** tool. Create a rectangle selection with a width of 225 and a height of 380. There is no need to be exact.

2. Go to the colors palette and choose the following color for the foreground color, and then click on **OK**.

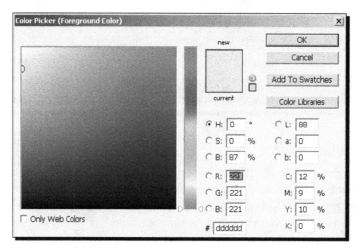

3. Go to the menu bar and choose **Edit | Stroke | OK** with the stroke set at 1px. Then go to the menu bar and choose **Select | Deselect**. You have just made the outline for your block.

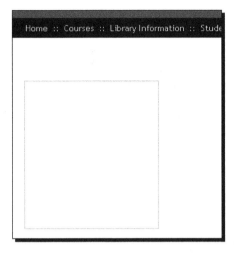

4. Create a new layer and click on the **Rectangular Marquee** tool and create a rectangle of 218 x 60 pixels.

5. Go to the file menu and choose **Select | Modify | Smooth**, and then the **Sample Radius** to 5px.

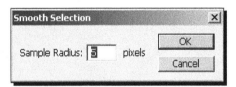

6. You should have something similar to the following screenshot:

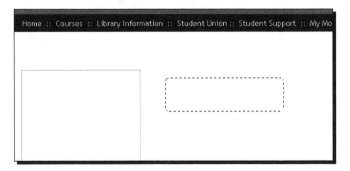

7. Now click on the gradient tool on the tools palette, but first make sure that your color chooser has the same colors as the following screenshot. The gray color is: #dddddd.

8. Now with the gradient toolbar showing, click on the gradient editor.

9. Choose the following settings from the dialog box that opens, ensuring that you click on the top left-hand box in the presets menu. It should have the same color (that is, gray) and state **Foreground to Background** in the tooltip. Then click on **OK**.

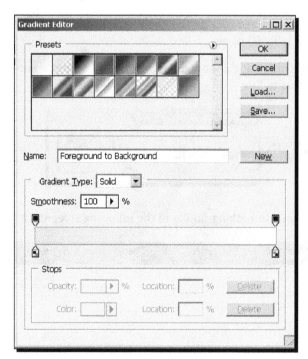

10. You will now have a cross hair cursor instead of an arrow. You should take this cross hair and draw a straight line right through the middle of your rounded corners box, from top to bottom. You will end up with something like the following screenshot:

11. Now go to the color chooser, and make gray the foreground color. Then go to the menu bar and choose **File | Edit | Stroke**, then click on **OK**, making sure that the stroke color is still the same gray. Then go to the menu bar again and choose **Select | Deselect**.

12. Now let's take a deep breath. Click on the rectangle marquee tool and make a selection over the last rounded box that you have just made with the gradient, just over half way down.

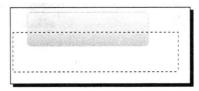

13. Then press *Ctrl + X* or choose menu option **File | Edit | Cut**.

14. Now click on the move tool on the tools menu and drag the block header that you have just made onto the top of the block that you made earlier.

What just happened?

Well, that was a tough one if you haven't had any Photoshop experience, wasn't it? You have learned how to create the graphics for your blocks that you will use in your Moodle theme later in this book. If you haven't had any Photoshop experience, then you should be getting familiar with the different tools and techniques that are used to create web graphics.

It is worth pointing out at this stage that if you had any issues with creating the required gradient then just go back to it and keep trying until you get it right or until you get a gradient that you like. This gradient will be saved by Photoshop so that you can use it for other design elements.

Have a go hero – you are on your own

Now that you have finished this chapter, you know why you should first think about the planning of any Moodle theme project, and will perhaps consider using Photoshop as a method by which you can visualize your planned theme. You might have also noticed that you didn't finish your Moodle theme design scamp. Well, this was intentional, as you are now going to do it alone and see if you can finish it.

Have a go hero – filling in the gaps

By using what you have learned so far, add some block header text to the block that you created in Photoshop. Just copy a current block's header from your Moodle site and try to make the color scheme and font type match your finished design scamp. Try using *Trebuchet MS* as the link font and #a1b2f0 as the color. Also, make it bold and choose a different link color for the roll-over and simulate this in Photoshop by making one of the links a different color.

Have a go hero – making the other blocks

Have a look at your Moodle site and re-create all of the blocks in your Photoshop mockup by reusing layers from it. You created only one sample block in this chapter, so you can do the rest. You can create a duplicate layer by clicking on the layer in the layers palette and then right-clicking and choosing **Duplicate layer**. You will be amazed how quick it is to produce all of the blocks that Moodle will have. This will help you visualize the end result well before you do any coding.

Summary

In this chapter, you have learned how important it is to plan ahead with Moodle theming. You now understand the importance of proper project management, and how and when you should create milestones in the theming process. You have also learned the basics of creating design scamps by using graphics manipulation software, and have been why this is a useful process.

Specifically, we covered:

◆ The importance of knowing your audience when theming for different groups of people

◆ The importance of gathering our assets, and what questions we should be asking ourselves

◆ Using paper and wireframing to help us visualize our planned Moodle theme design

◆ Using graphics software to further visualize a design so that you can build a complete mockup of our planned theme

Now that you've learned about the planning stages of creating Moodle themes, let's move on to *Chapter 7, First Steps: Creating Your First Complete Moodle Theme*, where you will put to use the knowledge that you have gained while working through this book so far, in order to create your new theme.

7

First Steps: Creating your First Complete Moodle Theme

In Chapter 7, you will start the process of creating your first complete Moodle theme. You will learn a little more about themes, parent themes, and how to set these in the theme's `config.php` file (not the one in Moodle's root folder). You will also learn that you can choose a theme from the default themes to base your theme on, and learn how to make your changes over the base theme.

In this chapter, we shall cover:

- Indentifying a base theme to use
- Making a copy of our theme
- Renaming the theme's directory
- Editing the theme's config file
- Making our first changes
- Alternative theme setups

So let's crack on...

Creating a new theme

Finding a base theme to create your Moodle theme on is the first thing that you need to do. There are, however, various ways to do this; you can make a copy of the *standard* theme and rename it as you did in part one of this book, or you can use a parent theme that is also based on the *standard* theme.

The important point here is that the *standard* theme that comes with Moodle is the cornerstone of the Moodle theming process. Every other Moodle theme should be based upon this theme, and would normally describe the differences from the *standard* theme. In part one of this book, we simply made a new theme by copying the *standard* theme's folder and renaming it. Although this method does work and is a simple way to get started with Moodle theming, it does cause problems as new features could get added to Moodle that might cause your theme to display or function incorrectly. The *standard* theme will always be updated before a new release of Moodle is launched. So if you do choose to make a copy of the *standard* theme and change its styles, it would be best to make sure that you use a parent theme as well. In this way, the parent theme will be your base theme along with the changes that you make to your copy of the *standard* theme.

However, there is another way of creating your first theme, and that is to create a copy of a theme that is very close to the *standard* theme, such as *standardwhite*, and use this as your theme. Moodle will then use the *standard* theme as its base theme and apply any changes that you make to the *standardwhite* theme on the top (parent). All we are doing is describing the differences between the *standard* and the *standardwhite* themes. This is better because Moodle developers will sometimes make changes to the *standard* theme to be up-to-date with new Moodle features. This means that on each Moodle update, your `standard` theme folder will be updated automatically, thus avoiding any nasty display problems being caused by Moodle updates.

The way by which you configure Moodle themes is completely up to you. If you see a theme that is nearly what you want and there aren't really many changes needed, then using a parent theme makes sense, as most of the styles that you require have already been written. However, if you want to create a theme that is completely different from any other theme or wish to really get into Moodle theming, then using a copy of one of the standard sheets would be best.

So let's get on and see what the differences are when using different theme setups, and see what effect these different methods have on the theming process.

Time for action – copying the standard theme

1. Browse to your `theme` folder in `C:\Program Files\Apache Software Foundation\Apache 2.2\htdocs\theme`.

2. Copy the `standard` theme by right-clicking on the theme's folder and choosing **Copy**.

3. Paste the copied theme into the `theme` directory (the same directory that you are currently in).

4. Rename the `copy of standard` folder to `blackandblue` or any other name that you wish to choose (remember not to use capitals or spaces).

5. Open your Moodle site and navigate to **Site Administration | Appearance | Themes | Theme Selector**, and choose the `blackandblue` theme that you have just created.

You might have noticed that the theme shown in the preceding screenshot has a header that says **Black and Blue theme**. This is because I have added this to the **Full site name** in the **Front Page settings** page.

So what you are looking at here is a copy of the *standard* theme to which you can start to make changes. However, because this is a copy of the *standard* theme, it will not be updated when new features are added to Moodle. So in this case, you will need to make your theme use a parent theme that does use the proper standard theme as its base.

Time for action – setting a parent theme

1. Open your web browser and navigate to your Moodle site and log in as the administrator.

2. Go to **Site Administration | Appearance | Themes | Theme Selector** and choose your *blackandblue* theme if it is not already selected.

3. Browse to the root of your `blackandblue` folder, right-click on the `config.php` file, and choose **Open with | WordPad**.

4. You need to make four changes to this file so that you can use this theme and a parent theme while ensuring that you still use the default *standard* theme as your base. Here are the changes:

```
$THEME->sheets = array('user_styles');
$THEME->standardsheets = true;
$THEME->parent = 'autumn';
$THEME->parentsheets = array('styles');
```

Let's look at each of these statements, in turn.

```
$THEME->sheets = array('user_styles');
```

This contains the names of all of the stylesheet files that you want to include in this theme, and in what order you want to use them. You will have only one stylesheet for your *blackandblue* theme, namely `user_styles`.

```
$THEME->standardsheets = true;
```

This parameter is used to include the *standard* theme's stylesheets. If it is set to `True`, it will use all of the stylesheets in the standard theme. Alternatively, it can be set as an array in order to load individual stylesheets in whatever order is required. We have set this to `True`, so we will use all of the stylesheets of the *standard* theme.

```
$THEME->parent = 'autumn';
```

This variable can be set to use a theme as the parent theme, which is included before the current theme. This will make it easier to make changes to another theme without having to change the actual files.

```
$THEME->parentsheets = array('styles');
```

This variable can be used to choose either all of the parent theme's stylesheets or individual files. It has been set to include the `styles.css` file from the parent theme, namely *autumn*. Because there is only one stylesheet in the *Autumn* theme, you can set this variable to `True`. Either way, you will have the same outcome.

5. Save `\theme\blackandblue\config.php`, and refresh your web browser window. You should see something similar to the following screenshot. Note that your blocks may be different to the ones below, but you can ignore this.

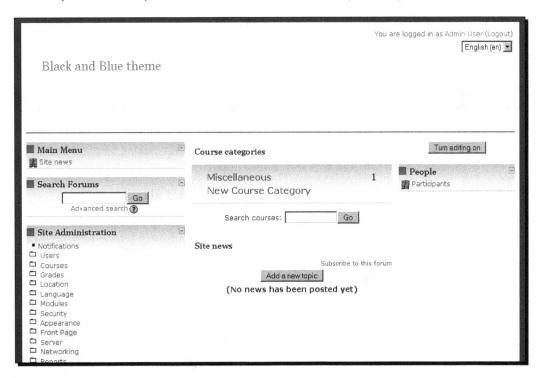

What just happened?

Okay, so now you have a copy of the *standard* theme that uses the *Autumn* theme (by Patrick Malley) as its parent. You might have noticed that the header isn't correct and that the proper *Autumn* theme header isn't showing. Well, this is because you are essentially using the copy of the *standard* theme and that the header from this theme is the one that you see above. It's only the CSS files that are included in this hierarchy, so any HTML changes will not be seen until you edit your *standard* theme's `header.html` file.

Have a go hero – choose another parent theme

Go back and have a look through some of the themes on `Moodle.org` and download one that you like. Add this theme as a parent theme to your *blackandblue* theme's `config.php` file, but this time choose which stylesheets you want to use from that theme. The *Back to School* theme is a good one for this exercise, as its stylesheets are clearly labeled. So you can choose to use the layouts and fonts' stylesheets, but not the color, for instance.

Copying the header and footer files

To show that you are using the *Autumn* theme's CSS files and the *standard* theme's HTML files, you can just go and copy the `header.html` and `footer.html` files from Patrick Malley's *Autumn* theme and paste them into your *blackandblue* theme's folder. Don't worry about overwriting your header and footer files, as you can always just copy them again from the actual *standard* theme folder.

Time for action – copying the header.html and footer.html files

1. Browse to the *Autumn* theme's folder and highlight both the `header.html` and `footer.html` files by holding down the *Ctrl* key and clicking on them both. Right-click on the selected files and choose **Copy**.

2. Browse to your *blackandblue* theme's folder, right-click, and choose **Paste**.

3. Go back to your browser window and press the *F5* button to refresh the page. You will now see the full *Autumn* theme.

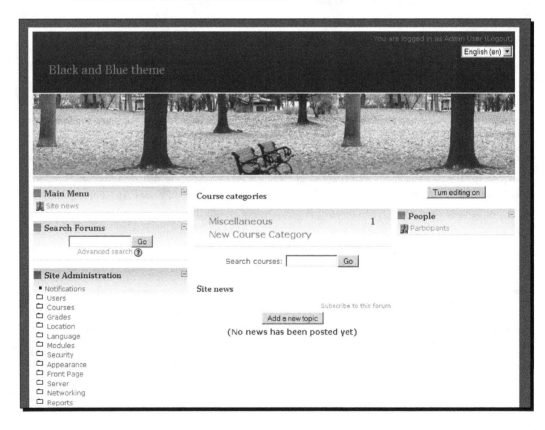

What just happened?

You have copied the *autumn* theme's `header.html` and `footer.html` files into your *blackandblue* theme, so you can see the full *Autumn* theme working. You probably will not actually use the `header.html` and `footer.html` files that you just copied, as this was just an example of how the Moodle theming process works.

So you now have an unmodified copy of the *standard* theme called *blackandblue*, which is using the *autumn* theme as its parent theme. All you need to do now to make changes to this theme is to edit your CSS file in the *blackandblue* theme folder.

Theme folder housework

However, there are a couple of things that you need to do first, as you have an exact copy of the *standard* theme apart from the `header.html` and `footer.html` files. This copied folder has files that you do not need, as the only file that you set for your theme to use was the `user_styles.css` file in the `config.php` file earlier. This was the first change that you made:

```
$THEME->sheets = array('user_styles');
```

The `user_styles.css` file does not exist in your *blackandblue* theme's folder, so you will need to create it. You will also need to delete any other CSS files that are present, as your new *blackandblue* theme will use only one stylesheet, namely the `user_styles.css` file that you will be creating in the following sections.

Time for action – creating our stylesheet

1. Right-click anywhere in your `blackandblue` folder and choose **New | Text Document**.

2. Rename this text document to `user_styles.css` by right-clicking again and choosing **Rename**.

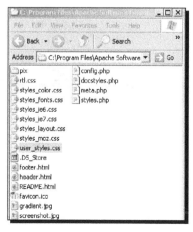

Time for action – deleting CSS files that we don't need

1. Delete the following CSS files by selecting them and then right-clicking on the selected files and choosing **Delete**.

- ❑ styles_color.css
- ❑ styles_fonts.css
- ❑ styles_ie6.css
- ❑ styles_ie7.css
- ❑ styles_layout.css
- ❑ styles_moz.css

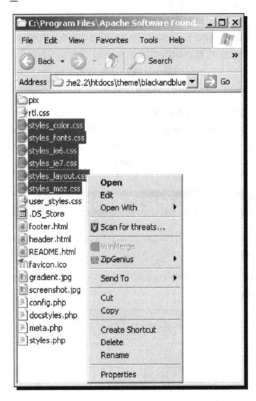

What just happened?

In the last two tasks, you created an empty CSS file called user_styles.css in your *blackandblue* theme's folder. You then deleted all of the CSS files in your *blackandblue* theme's folder, as you will no longer need them. Remember, these are just copies of the CSS files in the *standard* theme folder and you have set your theme to use the *standard* theme as its base in the *blackandblue* theme's config.php file.

Let's make some changes

Now you have set up your theme the way that you want it, that is, you are using your own *blackandblue* theme by using the *standard* theme as a base and the *Autumn* theme as the parent. Move on and make a few changes to your `user_styles.css` file so that you can see what effect this has on your theme, and check that all of your `config.php` file's settings are correct. Remember that all of the current styles are being inherited from the *Autumn* theme.

Time for action – checking our setup

1. Open up your Moodle site with the current theme (which should be *blackandblue* but looks like the *Autumn* theme).

2. Navigate to your *blackandblue* theme's folder, right-click on the `user_styles.css` file, and choose **Open**. This file should be completely blank.

3. Type in the following line of CSS for the body element, and then save the file:

```
body {
background: #000000;
}
```

4. Now refresh your browser window. You will see that the background is now black.

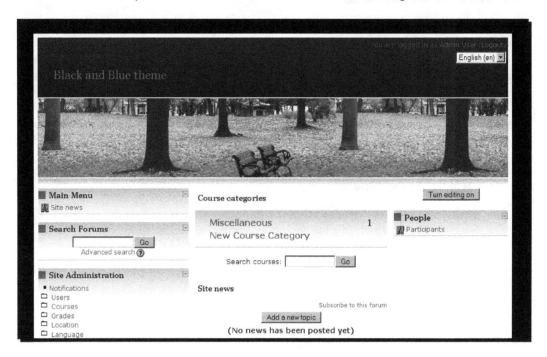

Note: When using Firebug to identify styles that are being used, it might not always be obvious where they are or which style is controlling that element of the page. An example of this is the `body {background: #000000;}` code that we just pasted in our `user_styles.css` file. If we had used Firebug to indentify that style, we would not have found it. Instead, I just took a look at the CSS file from the *Autumn* theme. What I am trying to say here is that there will always be an element of poking around and trial and error.

What just happened?

All seems fine there, doesn't it? You have added one style declaration to your empty `user_styles.css` file to change the background color, and have checked the changes in your browser. You now know how the parent themes work and know that you only need to copy the styles from Firebug into your `user_styles.css` file and edit the style declarations that need to be changed.

Let's make one more change, just so that we feel a little more comfortable with what we are doing. We are now going to change the background on the header and replace the gray gradient background image with a solid black color. To do this, we will be using Firebug to find the CSS statements. We will then copy and paste these into our `user_styles.css` file and finally edit the CSS declaration to achieve the desired result.

Time for action – one more change

1. Open up your Moodle site with the current theme (which should be *blackandblue* but looks like *Autumn*).

2. Open Firebug by clicking on the **Bug** icon.

3. Remember to click on the **Inspect** icon on the left-hand side of your Firebug window.

4. Roll your mouse over the header section, as set out in the following screenshot, and you should see a blue outline.

5. Check the resultant CSS code in the right-hand firebug window; it should look like the one in the next screenshot. The top six lines are the ones that we are after.

```
Style ▼   Layout   DOM
                                              styles.php (line 97)
#header-home .headerimg2, #header {
    -moz-background-clip: border;
    -moz-background-inline-policy: continuous;
⊘   -moz-background-origin: padding;
    background: #2D2D2D url(pix/topbg.gif) repeat-x scroll left top;
}
                                              styles.php (line 92)
#header-home .headerimg2 {
    height: 112px;
    margin-bottom: 2px;
}
Inherited from body#site-index.course
```

6. Highlight the top six lines of CSS, right-click on them, and choose **Copy**.

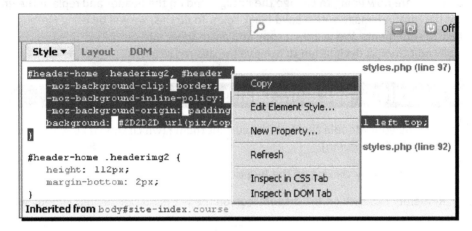

7. Open your user_styles.css file once again, place your cursor below the background declaration, and then choose **Paste**.

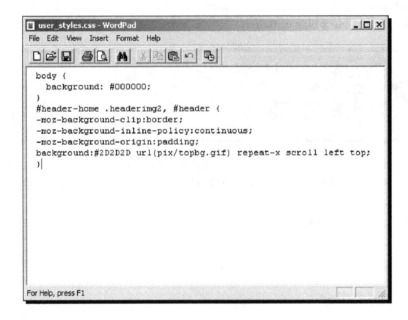

8. Delete everything that you copied except for the part of the last line as seen below:

background:#000000;

9. Refresh your browser window and you should have replaced the gray-to-black gradient background image to a solid black color.

What just happened?

In this task, you have made another small change to your `user_styles.css` file and have successfully changed a part of the header's background from a gradient image to a solid color. You have also covered some of the techniques learned in earlier chapters to copy and paste styles (by using Firebug) into your `user_styles.css` file in your `theme` directory.

Another theme setup

In this section, we will cover in a little more detail some of the complexities surrounding themes, with specific reference to parent themes and the importance of using the *standard* theme as the base of any theme that you create. There are, however, other methods of creating themes, one of which we are going to have a look at next.

This is important, as although we covered themes in an earlier chapter of this book, we didn't cover them in sufficient detail for us to know how exactly they work. This chapter (and the entire book of course) is about becoming completely familiar with Moodle's theming process. So for these reasons, we are going to have a look at another theming method.

This next method is the way that I prefer, as it gives me complete control over my theme; and lets me start with a very basic theme that is included with Moodle. In this theme setup, we will not be using parent themes at all and will be basing our theme on the *standard* theme and using the *standardwhite* theme to layer on top of it. We will then use the *standardwhite* theme to work from, making changes to this as we go along. Remember, we will not be using the *standardwhite* as a parent with this theming setup; rather we will be using it as our theme, minus a few files. The difference here is that instead of using:

OurTheme > ParentTheme > StandardTheme

We will be using:

OurTheme > StandardTheme

So let's continue with this theming method, as this will be the one that we continue with throughout the book.

Time for action – preparing our new theme

1. Navigate to your `htdocs\theme\blackandblue` folder, right-click on it, and choose **Copy**.

2. Paste this folder somewhere safe (maybe on your desktop), as you might want to use it later.

3. Go back to your `blackandblue` folder and delete all of the files inside it. Navigate to the `standardwhite` folder, and copy all of the files by selecting them all and then right-clicking and choosing **Copy**.

4. Navigate back to your *blackandblue* theme's folder, right-click inside it, and then choose **Paste**. Your folder should look like the following screenshot:

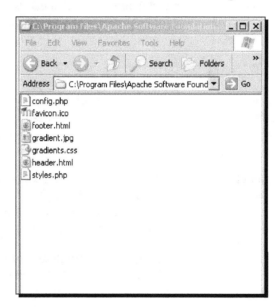

5. Right-click again and choose **New | Text Document**. Rename this text document to `user_styles.css`.

6. Right-click on the `config.php` file and choose **Open With | WordPad**.

7. Change the line:

```
$THEME->sheets = array('gradients');
```

To:

```
$THEME->sheets = array('user_styles');
```

This ensures that you will be using your own stylesheet in the *blackandblue* theme.

8. Save the `config.php` file, go back to your Moodle site, and refresh the browser window. You should see that your *blackandblue* theme changes to the following screenshot:

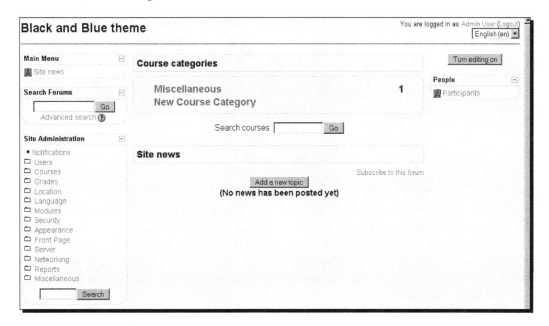

What just happened?

In this exercise, you have made a copy of your *blackandblue* theme and pasted this somewhere safe (because you might need this theme at a later stage) and then deleted all of the files in the `blackandblue` folder. You then made a copy of the *standardwhite* theme and pasted this theme into your now-empty *blackandblue* theme. You also changed the `config` file in your theme's folder to load the new `user_styles.css` file that you created.

Have a go hero – more advanced theming

Using what you have learned so far, go back and change the `config.php` file in your *blackandblue* theme's folder so that it loads only the `layout.css` from the standard theme, and see what happens. Think about why you would do this. The answer to this is that you might want only the layout of the standard theme and not the fonts and link colors. The more of the standard styles that you use, the more that you will have to overwrite at a later stage.

Summary

In this chapter, you have learned a lot more about themes and their relationship with each other. You should now understand the difference between a theme and a parent theme, and how you can use the Moodle theming process to load certain themes or even elements of these themes before your own theme's styles are used. You should also understand why you might use parent themes, and what would be the best method in any given situation.

Specifically, we covered:

- Creating a new theme from a copied current theme
- Setting a parent theme to use with our copied theme
- Why we might want to have a parent theme
- When not to use a parent theme

Now that you know how to mix and match different themes, and know how to get the most from the Moodle theming process, you shall use what you have learned to create your first complete theme. You will be using the *blackandblue* theme that you created at the end of this chapter and your design mockup created in *Chapter 6, Planning your Moodle Theme* to start to shape your theme into something that will be useable, accessible, and easily changeable at a later stage.

8
Creating your Moodle Theme from your Mockup: Slice and Dice

In Chapter 8, you will start to "slice and dice", which will take you through a series of exercises so that you can edit the header and footer of your Moodle theme to match that of the mockup that was created in the planning stage. This chapter will also take you through the process of changing all of the links, fonts, headings, and background, and then continue on to changing the theme's icons and testing the changes you have made.

In this chapter, we shall cover:

- ◆ Creating the header
- ◆ Creating the footer
- ◆ Setting the font styles
- ◆ Setting the link styles
- ◆ Setting the background color
- ◆ Changing the icons
- ◆ Testing our changes

So let's get on with it...

Creating the header

The first thing that you need to do in order to create your header from the design mockup that was created in *Chapter 6, Planning your Moodle Theme* is to get your working environment set up properly. In most cases, this simply involves opening the appropriate programs, so that you can work a little more quickly. If you cast your mind back, you should remember that you used Adobe Photoshop (or your favorite graphics manipulation software program) to create the graphics for your *blackandblue* theme. You also used Mozilla Firefox as your web browser, and nothing more than WordPad to create the HTML and CSS code. So go ahead and open these programs.

Time for action – setting the header size and background color

1. Open the design mockup that you created in *Chapter 6, Planning your Moodle Theme* by using Adobe Photoshop.

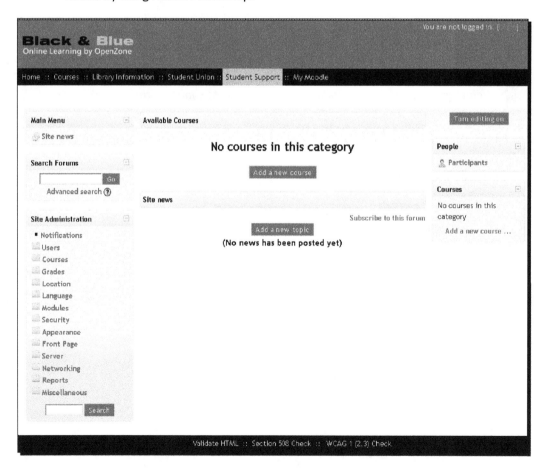

Mine looks something like the preceding screenshot, and so should yours if you completed the last chapter, including the *Have a go hero* sections. If it doesn't, it is maybe because you didn't complete the whole chapter or you didn't get around to creating all the blocks. Don't worry too much, as we only need to create the CSS for one block to create them all in Moodle.

2. Click on the Rectangular Marquee tool.

3. Drag a selection area from the top of the blue header to the bottom, and don't worry too much about the width, as you are measuring only the height.

4. Look at the **Info** palette on the right-hand side of your screen to get the exact height in pixels. You should see figures for the width and the height. As you can see in the following screenshot, the height is 91px.

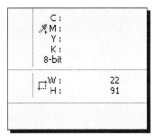

5. Open Firefox and navigate to your local Moodle site. Make sure that your *blackandblue* theme is loaded. If not, please choose this theme.

6. Open Firebug by clicking on the **Bug** icon. Then click on the **Inspect** icon on the top left-hand side of Firebug and hover your mouse over the header text, as seen in the screenshot below:

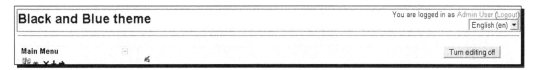

7. Copy the code that is highlighted in the following screenshot from the right-hand Firebug window.

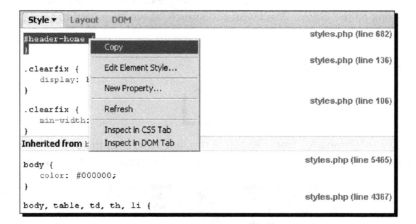

8. Paste this code into your `user_styles.css` file in your *blackandblue* theme's folder, and add the rest of the code shown below.

We added a second CSS class here so that the inner page headers are the same as the home page header.

9. Now refresh the browser window, and the header should be slightly larger in height. Check to see if any inner pages' headers are of the same height by clicking on any link.

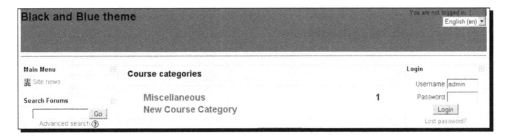

What just happened?

You measured your header from your design mockup that was created in *Chapter 6, Planning your Moodle Theme*, and set your first styles in the user_styles.css file for your theme. The result is that your header is now the same height that you made it in the mockup, and also has the same background color as your mockup.

You now need to set the margins because you have a white border around the edge of the page that you need to get rid of, and then you need to add your *blackandblue* logo.

Time for action – setting the margins and adding a logo

1. Using Firebug, roll your mouse over the blue header section until you get a blue line around the whole page. This is known as selecting a page element in Firebug.

We used the **Rectangular Marquee** tool in Photoshop to measure the height of our header. There is a specific measurement tool on the **Tools** palette, but it is rather difficult to use. Feel free to try it out if you would rather use the proper tools for the job. Also, when you selected the area you needed to measure, you might have found it a little difficult. If so, try zooming in to the design by pressing *Ctrl* and + on your keyboard.

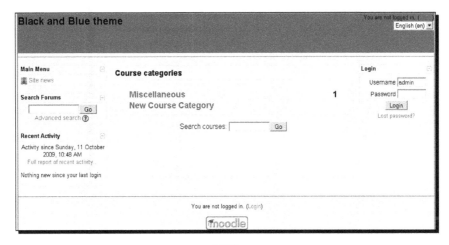

2. Now highlight the `body` class in the right-hand Firebug window and choose **Copy**, as shown in the following screenshot:

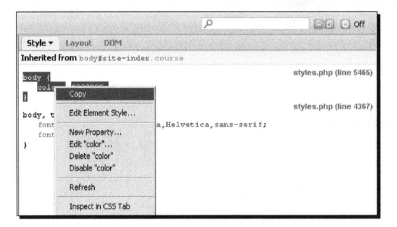

3. Open your `user_styles.css` file and paste this text above the other CSS code. Then add the following line of CSS:

```
margin:0px;
```

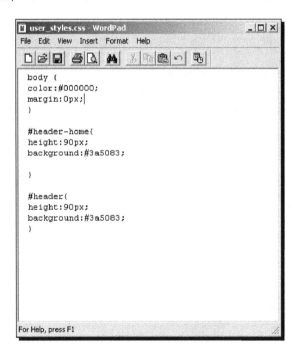

4. Now refresh your browser window, and you should see something similar to the following screenshot:

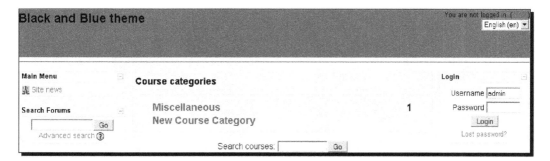

In the next part of this exercise, you will be using Adobe Photoshop again, to cut your logo from the *blackandblue* design mockup. You will also be editing the `header.html` file, so you can add your logo to your theme.

5. Start Adobe Photoshop and open your *blackandblue* design mockup.

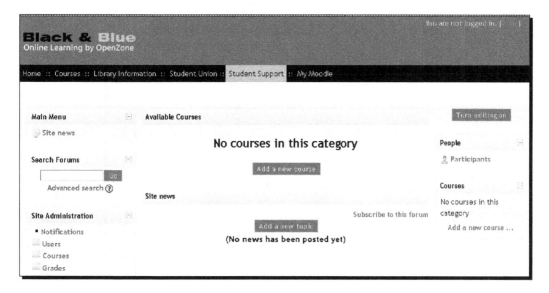

6. Click on the **Rectangular Marquee** tool.

7. Drag your mouse over the **Black & Blue** logo, as seen below:

8. Choose **Edit | Copy Merged** from the menu bar in Photoshop.

9. Then choose menu option **File | New**, and then click on **OK**.

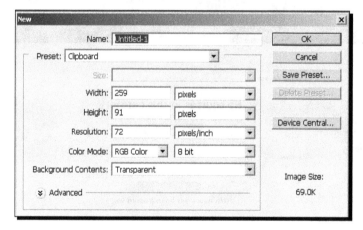

10. Next select menu option **Edit | Paste**.

11. Go to the menu bar and choose **Save for Web and Devices** and choose the same options as set out in the image below:

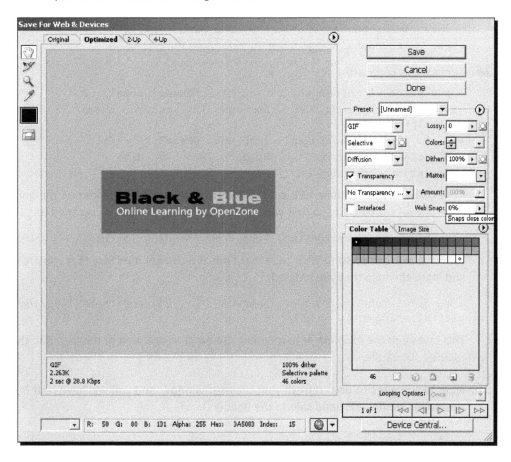

12. Click on the **Save** button, and save the image as `logo.gif` to the root of your theme folder.

Now take a deep breath, because you now need to continue editing your `header.html` file so that you can use the logo that was just created. For this part of the exercise, you are going to remove the generated header text and simply replace this with the logo that you just created.

13. Navigate to your *blackandblue* theme's folder and open your `header.html` file with WordPad.

14. Find the following section of code:

```
<?php print_container_start(true, '', 'header-home'); ?>
<h1 class="headermain"><?php echo $heading ?></h1>
  <div class="headermenu"><?php echo $menu ?></div>
<?php print_container_end(); ?>
```

15. Replace this code with:

```
<?php print_container_start(true, '', 'header-home'); ?>
<img src="<?php echo $CFG->themewww .'/'. current_theme() ?>/logo.
gif" alt="logo" />
<!--<h1 class="headermain"><?php echo $heading ?></h1>-->
  <div class="headermenu"><?php echo $menu ?></div>
<?php print_container_end(); ?>
```

Note that you have commented out the lines that generate the header on the home page of your Moodle site so that you can still use this code later if you need to.

```
<!--<h1 class="headermain"><?php echo $heading ?></h1>-->
```

You have also added some PHP code that finds the current directory that you are in and loads the logo that you created.

```
<img src="<?php echo $CFG->themewww .'/'. current_theme() ?>/logo.
gif" alt="logo" />
```

This saves you the problem of hardcoding the exact image path of the logo into the `header.html` file.

16. Now all you need to do is refresh your browser window, and you will have your logo positioned on the left-hand side of the header.

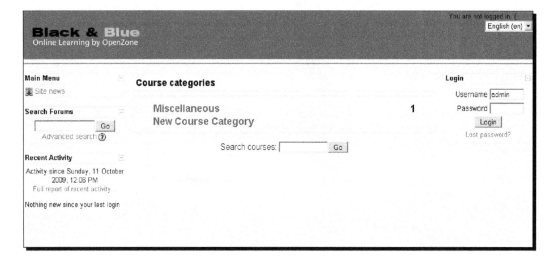

What just happened?

In this exercise, you learned how to set the margins of your theme to zero and go through all of the steps that were necessary to "slice and dice" your logo from the design mockup that was created in *Chapter 6, Planning Your Moodle Theme*. Then you edited your `header.html` file and added the code required to load your logo in place of the Moodle-generated header text. You have also learned how to comment out the Moodle heading part of the code so that it can be reused at a later stage if necessary.

Have a go hero – moving the login info link

You may have also noticed that the login info link is right up against the top right-hand side. This could really do with some padding so it's not right up to the edge. With what you have already learned, and using Firebug, give this area some padding. A clue on how to do this is set out below:

```
.headermenu
```

Have a go hero – making the inner page headers the same as the home page

If you navigate anywhere else on your Moodle site, you will notice that the inner pages do not have the same features that we have just built. Copy all the features from the front page into the inner pages. This is much easier than you think, and requires only one **Copy** and **Paste** from the `header.html` file.

Creating the menu

Let's continue from where you left off, but this time you will be creating the menu for your Moodle theme. To create this menu, you will again need to make some changes to your `header.html` file, and will also be adding some CSS to your `user_styles.css` file. There is a little trick performed here insofar as you will be creating a new file called `menu.php` and calling this file with a small piece of PHP code that you will add to the `header.html` file.

Time for action – creating the menu.php file

1. Open up WordPad, or if it is already open just go to the menu bar and choose **File | New**.

2. Type the following lines of code into your newly created `menu.php` file:

```
<a href="<?php echo $CFG->wwwroot; ?>"
    title="Home">Home</a> :: 
```

```
<a href="<?php echo $CFG->wwwroot; ?>/course/index.php"
   title="Courses">Courses</a> :: 
<a href="<?php echo $CFG->wwwroot;?>/calendar/view.php?view=month"
   title="Calendar">Calendar</a> :: 
```

3. Save this file as menu.php.

What just happened?

You created a PHP file called menu.php, which includes links to the home, calendar, and courses pages in Moodle. This little file will make it much easier to add links at a later stage to Moodle, as you will not have to edit the header.html file. You will be including the menu.php file created in the menu block, next.

Time for action – creating the menu block

1. Open your header.html file and find the following code:

```
<?php print_container_start(true, '', 'header-home'); ?>
<img src="<?php echo $CFG->themewww .'/'. current_theme() ?>/logo.
gif" alt="logo" />
<!--    <h1 class="headermain"><?php echo $heading ?></h1>-->
  <div class="headermenu"><?php echo $menu ?></div>
<?php print_container_end(); ?>
```

2. Replace this with:

```
<?php print_container_start(true, '', 'header-home'); ?>
<img src="<?php echo $CFG->themewww .'/'. current_theme() ?>/logo.
gif" alt="logo" />
  <!--<h1 class="headermain"><?php echo $heading ?></h1>-->
  <div class="headermenu"><?php echo $menu ?></div>
  <div id="menubox"><?php include 'menu.php'; ?></div> - adds the
menu.php to the header
<?php print_container_end(); ?>
```

3. Refresh your browser window, and nothing should have happened. If it did, then make sure that all of the above code is present in your header.html file.

4. Open your user_styles.css file from within your theme folder, and add the following CSS code:

```
#menubox
{
 background-color:#000000; - changes the background color to black
 height:32px; - Gives the menu box a height of 32 pixels
}
```

Your `user_styles.css` file should now look like this:

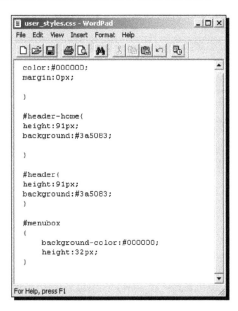

5. Now that you have added the menu bar to the header, you will need to make the `header-home` CSS larger to accommodate it. So to do this, just add the 91px for the #header-home class with the 23px for the #menubox, and you come up with 123px. Now just change the #header-home and the #header height to 123px ,as seen below:

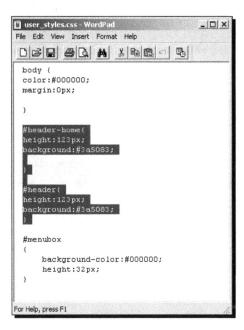

6. Open the `header.html` file, remove the `<hr>` tag highlighted in the following screenshot, and then save your changes.

```
header.html - WordPad
File  Edit  View  Insert  Format  Help

<?php //Accessibility: 'headermain' is now H1, see theme/standard/styles_layout.css: .headermain
    if ($home) {  // This is what gets printed on the home page only
?>
    <?php print_container_start(true, '', 'header-home'); ?>
    <img src="<?php echo $CFG->themewww .'/'. current_theme() ?>/logo.gif" alt="logo" />
    <!--<h1 class="headermain"><?php echo $heading ?></h1>-->
    <div class="headermenu"><?php echo $menu ?></div>
    <div id="menubox"></div>
    <?php print_container_end(); ?>

<?php } else if ($heading) {  // This is what gets printed on any other page with a heading
?>
    <?php print_container_start(true, '', 'header'); ?>
        <h1 class="headermain"><?php echo $heading ?></h1>
        <div class="headermenu"><?php echo $menu ?></div>
    <?php print_container_end(); ?>
<?php } ?>
<?php //Accessibility: breadcrumb trail/navbar now a DIV, not a table.
    if ($navigation) { // This is the navigation bar with breadcrumbs  ?>
    <div class="navbar clearfix">
        <div class="breadcrumb"><?php print_navigation($navigation); ?></div>
        <div class="navbutton"><?php echo $button; ?></div>
    </div>
<?php } else if ($heading) { // If no navigation, but a heading, then print a line
?>
<?php } ?>
<hr>
    <!-- END OF HEADER -->
    <?php print_container_start(true, '', 'content'); ?>

For Help, press F1
```

7. Refresh your browser, and your theme header should look like the following screenshot:

These links will change once you have your theme up and running, and can be set to whatever you will need. All you have to do is navigate to any page of Moodle and then cut the URL from the browser's address bar and paste it into one of the `<a href>` lines above. Or, of course, you can create a totally new page.

Not perfect, I think you will agree, but we will be changing the link colors and fonts a little later.

What just happened?

In the previous exercise, you created the menu bar from your design mockup by using HTML and CSS.

You might have noticed in the last task that you added a small piece of PHP code. This code is used to call a separate file so that you can add the menu items to this file and subsequently keep them out of your `header.html` file. The reason why we do this is to keep the `header.html` file tidy and also to provide an easy way to add menu links without needing to edit this file.

Creating the footer

In the next part of this chapter, you will be creating the footer from your design mockup. This part should be a little easier than the header section, as there will be far fewer steps needed. If you now have a quick look at the design mockup that you created, you can visualize what changes you need to make to the footer section. After this you will remove the login info link and the Moodle logo.

Time for action – creating the footer bar

1. Start Adobe Photoshop, and open the design mockup that you created.

It's just a simple black bar—an exact copy of the menu bar, actually.

2. Open the `footer.html` file from your *blackandblue* theme folder with WordPad.

3. Comment out the following PHP code from this file, and then save your changes:

```
/*echo $loggedinas;
echo $homelink;*/
```

4. Refresh your browser, and the login info link and the Moodle logo should have disappeared. (This part has been covered in *Chapter 3, Customizing the Header and Footer*).

5. Comment out the following PHP code in order to delete the line that runs across the bottom of your footer:

```
/*echo "<hr />";*/
```

6. Now you need to insert the following code at the very top of your `footer.html` file, and then save your changes. This will add a black bar across the footer to match the header menu bar.

```
<div id="menubox"></div>
```

7. Refresh your browser, and check the results. Your page should be similar to the one shown in the next screenshot:

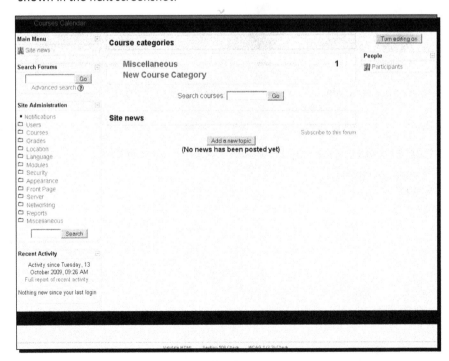

What just happened?

In this exercise, you created your footer bar for your *blackandblue* theme. You commented out the login info link and the Moodle logo, so that you can add them back (if required) at a later stage. You also added a simple `<div>` tag and reused the `#menubox` ID that was defined in the `user_styles.css` file, to create a copy of the menu bar.

Remember that you have already defined a `#menubox` ID in your `user_styles.css` file when you created the top menu, so this doesn't need to be done again; you just reuse this for your footer bar. Also, if you need any links placed in the footer bar, you can place them between the `<div>` tags, or use a similar approach to the one that you used in the menu bar—that is, use a PHP include statement and create the file as a separate `footermenu.php` file.

Setting the font and link styles

In this section, you will be changing the font and link styles to the same as you defined in your design mockup in *Chapter 6, Planning your Moodle Theme*. If you cast your minds back to *Chapter 2, Moodle Themes*, you will remember that you used *Trebuchet MS* as your font for this design. So the first task is to set the body font, which will define the font used throughout the theme and consequently throughout your Moodle site.

Time for action – setting the body font

1. Open the `user_styles.css` file in the root of your *blackandblue* theme's folder.

2. Open the Moodle site by using Firefox and open Firebug (you should know how to do this by now).

3. Click on the **Inspect** icon on the top left-hand side of Firebug, and hover your mouse pointer over some plain text (not links). I have chosen the **Search courses** text in the middle of the page.

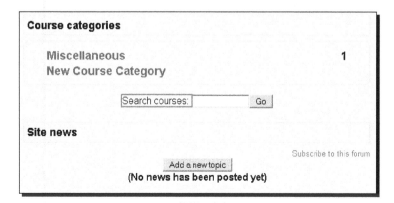

4. Now you need to check the right-hand Firebug window. You might notice that this is slightly different than previous examples, as the only font style visible isn't at the top. This is because all of the different text elements are inherited from the body class, as seen in the following screenshot:

5. Right-click on the body class highlighted above, and choose **Copy**.

6. Open your user_styles.css file. Note that you already have a body class defined in your stylesheet.

7. Add the copied CSS statements to the already-defined body class, and then change the first font in the font-family list to *Trebuchet MS,* and then save your changes. See the next screenshot:

8. Refresh your browser, and all the fonts on the page should have changed from *Arial* to *Trebuchet MS*.

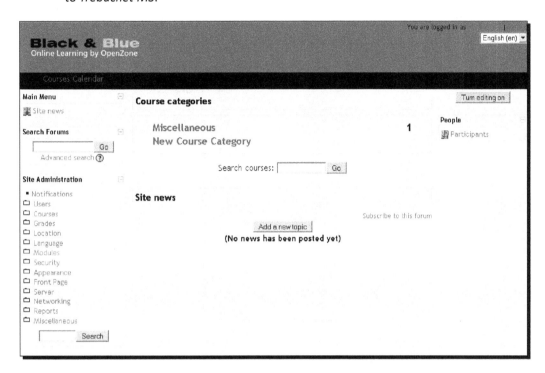

What just happened?

In this exercise, you have simply changed the font that your *blackandblue* theme uses from the *Arial* font to *Trebuchet MS*.

Now it's time to change your link styles to the styles that you defined in your design mockup. The font type was set to the same style as your body font. So you can leave this style as it is, and just change the color and weight of your link styles.

Have a go hero – styling the login info link

When you set about styling the links, you didn't style the login info link on the top right-hand corner. This still has links that are dark blue and therefore cannot be seen. Using what you have learned so far, style these links so they are white. A clue as to how to do this is given below:

```
.headermenu a:link, .headermenu a:visited
```

Time for action – changing the link styles

1. Open up the `user_styles.css` file if it is not already open.

2. Open Firefox, then open Firebug, and click on the **Inspect** icon.

3. Hover your mouse over one of the links in the **Site Administration** block (make sure that you are logged in as an administrator).

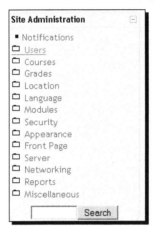

4. Copy the two top CSS classes as seen in the next screenshot (you will need to copy these separately) and paste them into the bottom of your `user_styles.css` file.

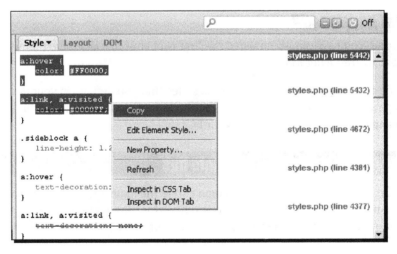

5. If you look back to the *Have a go hero* section in *Chapter 6, Planning your Moodle Theme*, you should remember that you set the `font-color` to `#3a5083` and set the `font-weight` to bold. Now change the `a:link`, `a:visited`, and `a:hover` classes to match the next screenshot, and then save your changes.

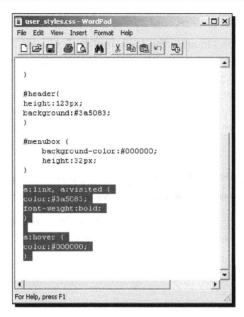

6. Refresh your browser, and check whether the changes have been successful; hover your mouse pointer over a link to check that it turns black.

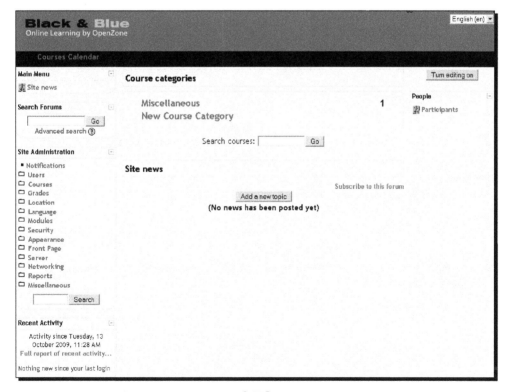

What just happened?

In the last two exercises, you changed the body font to *Trebuchet MS*, and changed the links' style to use the color #3a5083 for the link color and black for the link hover color. Your theme now is really starting to look like the one you created as a mockup in *Chapter 6, Planning your Moodle Theme*. But there is one last thing that you need to do in this section, and that is to make the menu font the same size and color as in your design mockup. You also need to align the text properly so that it is positioned vertically in the middle of the menu bar.

Time for action – changing the menu font style

1. Open the user_styles.css file and type the following lines of CSS into the bottom of the file, and then save your changes:

```
#menu a:link,a:active{
    font-weight:normal;
    color:#ffffff;
    text-decoration:none;
    font-size:92%;
}

#menu a:hover,a:visited {
    color:#3a5083;
}

#menu {
padding-left:20px;
}
```

2. Find the #menubox class and change the CSS statement so that it looks like the following code:

```
#menubox {
    background-color:#000000;
    height:32px;
    line-height:32px;
}
```

3. Open the menu.php file from the root of your theme folder, and wrap the existing code with:

```
<div id="menu">code</div>
```

as seen below, and then save your changes:

4. Refresh your browser to view the changes.

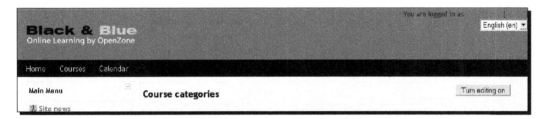

What just happened?

In this exercise, you wrapped the `menu.php` links in a `<div>` tag so that you could give them a CSS ID. You did this so that you could define some different-styled links for the menu than the rest of the links in your theme. You also added a `line-height` class to the `#menubox` class in order to center the text vertically within the menu bar. The results are that you have much cleaner-looking menu links. Finally, you added a `#menu` class so that you could add a `left-padding` of 20px.

Changing the icons

Another design change that you might want to implement is to replace the icons, as the standard ones are a little drab. The easiest way to do this is to copy an entire `pix` folder from another theme and paste it into your theme's folder. Another way to it is to find a great set of icons and replace the icons in your theme one-by-one. The next exercise will introduce you to both methods.

Time for action – changing the icon set

1. Browse to another theme that has been installed by default in Moodle. This is important as you might break copyright laws if you use someone else's icon sets. Try the *chameleon* theme for starters.

2. Make a backup of the entire *blackandblue* folder and paste this onto your desktop.

3. Copy the entire `pix` folder and paste it into your `blackandblue` folder.

4. Open your `config.php` file from the root of your theme's folder, and change the following line of code from:

   ```
   THEME->custompix = false;
   ```

   to:

   ```
   $THEME->custompix = true;
   ```

5. Refresh your browser, and hey presto: you have a new icon set.

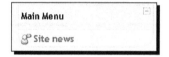

What just happened?

In the last exercise, you learned how to change the icon set by copying a `pix` folder from another theme and pasting this into the correct place in your own theme. You also learned how to change the theme's `config` file to tell the theme to use custom pictures. You achieved this by changing the following line of code from:

```
THEME->custompix = false;
```

to:

```
THEME->custompix = true;
```

Changing icons one at a time

As explained previously, the other method of changing your icons, which takes rather longer to do is, to change the icons one at a time. I actually prefer this method, as it enables me to choose really good icons as I go about my daily Moodle tasks. This can involve choosing icons from more than one Moodle icon set, or simply going and finding a great set of icons that you are allowed to use on the Internet.

With this method, you have to make sure that you are consistent in choosing icons, meaning that you should try to make sure that they look similar. You can find many icon websites on the Internet, but to get you going here are a few examples:

`http://www.maxpower.ca/`: Click on the free icon link in the menu bar

`http://www.kde-look.org/`: For Linux desktops, but some good ones nevertheless

`http://www.rad-e8.com/`: Stylized and minimalistic

`http://iconfactory.com/freeware/`: Great unique icons

Time for action – changing icons one at a time

1. Delete the `pix` folder that you copied in the last exercise.

2. Go to your desktop and find the backup of the `blackandblue` folder that you created in the *Changing the icons* section of this chapter. Copy the `pix` folder, and paste it back to the `blackandblue` folder that you are working with (`\themes\blackandblue`).

3. Find a good icon from either the Internet or another Moodle icon set.

4. Right-click on the icon that you want to replace in your *blackandblue* theme. For this task, choose one of the closed folder icons next to the links in the administration menu and select **Properties**.

5. To the right of the location line, you will see the icon's path and name. Remember this or write it down.

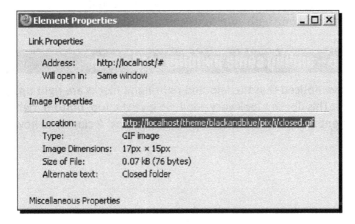

6. Locate the icon that you want to use and rename it to the same name as in the properties dialog box, and copy it to the same directory in your *blackandblue* theme's `pix` directory. In this case, it would be to your `pix\` directory. Say **Yes** when prompted to overwrite the icon that is already there.

7. Refresh your browser and your new icon should appear. You might need to press *Ctrl + F5* a couple of times, as these icons are often cached.

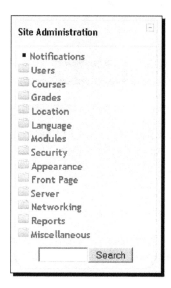

Now they look a lot better, don't they?

What just happened?

In this exercise, you learned how to change the icons individually by changing a single icon's filename to the same name as the icon it is replacing in the *blackandblue* theme's `pix` folder. You also learned how to determine what folder this icon would be stored in so that you can copy and replace the old one with your new icon.

Have a go hero – adding some padding to the page

You might also have noticed that the left- and right-hand blocks are right up against the edges of the page. This doesn't look very good. So give the top, bottom, right, and left edges of the content section of the page a padding of 20px. A clue as to how to do this is given below:

```
#content
```

Have a go hero – testing your changes

One task that I have repeatedly suggested throughout this book is that you test your changes as you go along. This means that on each change you should open Internet Explorer, Opera, Google Chrome, and Safari, and confirm that the changes have worked. Don't worry too much about tiny differences such as the way fonts look, because they will look different in Internet Explorer compared to Firefox. Just make sure that the main structural changes work.

If you find some issues, then it is likely that you have missed a } or made a syntactical error in your CSS.

Summary

In this chapter, you have really been getting stuck in to creating your theme. You have created the header and footer and added your own logo. You have also changed the fonts and set the link styles throughout your Moodle site. You have learned how to create your own menu bar and add links to it. Finally, you have learned how to change the icons so that you can completely customize your theme.

Specifically, we covered:

- Modifying the header
- Creating the menu
- Creating the footer
- Setting the font and link styles
- Changing the icons

Now that you have made some good headway into creating your *blackandblue* theme, you can move on to getting right under the hood. In the next chapter, you will learn how to style the blocks including the background and block headers. You will also learn how to style the login screen and make the breadcrumb trail fit your theme's style.

9

Under the Hood: Style your Navigation, Login Screen, and Blocks

Chapter 9 will further develop the skills you learned in the previous chapter, and will show you how to change the look and feel of some more functional elements of Moodle. This will include elements such as the splash page login screen, the width and appearance of the sideblock headers, and sideblock content areas. You will also learn how to style the breadcrumb trail and test these changes in multiple browsers.

In this chapter, we shall cover:

- ◆ Styling the login screen
- ◆ Setting the width of the sideblocks
- ◆ Changing the appearance of the blocks
- ◆ Styling the breadcrumb trail
- ◆ Testing our changes

So let's get started...

Changing the login splash page

One thing that you might want to change with your theme is the login screen. Many Moodle administrators often miss this screen or leave it as it is. For the next exercise, you will be making only a small change to this screen, just to explore what can be done.

Time for action – opening the login page

1. Using your preferred browser, navigate to your Moodle site's home page.

2. Log in as the administrator.

3. Click on the **Logout** link on the top right-hand side of Moodle. This logs you out of Moodle and changes the login info link from **Logout** to **Login**.

4. Click on the **Login** link, and it will take you to the login page.

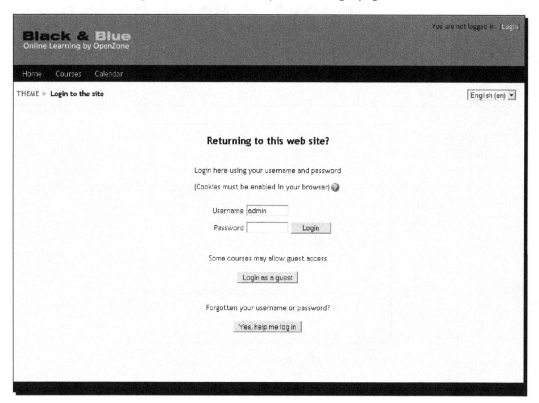

What just happened?

In this quick exercise, you have learned how to get to the login page of Moodle. This might sound very obvious, but you would be surprised to know how many people have finished a theme and have never visited this page, as they always use the login block instead.

Adding a border around the central box

As you can see there isn't really much to change here apart from maybe the border around the central box area. So let's get on with it, and add a border around this box.

Time for action – changing the border around the central box

1. In your browser, open Firebug and click on the **Inspect** icon on the left-hand side.

2. Hover your mouse over the central box so that the very outside of the box is highlighted, as seen below:

3. View the inspect window in Firebug in the right-hand pane. Slightly confusing, isn't it? This is because we have several `loginbox` styles listed.

An explanation of these styles is probably helpful. The top `.loginbox` style is to add the curved corner to the bottom of the box (this only works in Firefox). The two middle CSS styles just give the box its gray border. The bottom `.loginbox` style sets the width of the border, the width of the box, and its padding. You will need the first four styles here. So highlight each of the first four styles and copy them one at a time into the `user_styles.css` file, as seen below:

4. Change the following lines of CSS, and then save the `user_styles.css` file. This is the CSS file that you created for your *blackandblue* theme. It should be the only CSS file in this folder.

    ```
    .loginbox, .loginbox.twocolumns .loginpanel, .loginbox .subcontent
    {
    border-color:#DDDDDD;
    }
    ```

- Change the lines to:

```
.loginbox, .loginbox.twocolumns .loginpanel, .loginbox .subcontent
{
border-color:red;
}
```

5. Refresh the browser window and you should see that the border around the login box is red.

6. You changed the color of the border to red so that you could clearly see the changes that you have made. So now go back to your `user_styles.css` file, change the color to `#3a5083`, save the file, and then refresh your browser. You have now changed the color of the border to the same color as the header in your theme.

What just happened?

In the last exercise, you copied the `.loginbox` styles to your `user_styles.css` file and changed the border color of the central login box. You copied several `.loginbox` styles from Firebug to your `user_styles.css` file, but used only one of them. This is because there are several different styles that control the look and feel of the login box on the login screen. You will be learning at a later stage what the other CSS styles do.

Changing the width of the sideblocks

In this section, you are going to change the width of the sideblocks, and make the left-hand blocks slightly larger than the right. We have already described why and how we might do this, in *Chapter 5, Changing the Layout*. We also discussed that some blocks within Moodle such as the calendar block, have their widths set within their own code, so you must always approach this technique with caution, and should test thoroughly as you develop your theme.

Time for action – copying and pasting the width code from index.php to config.php

1. From **My Computer**, go to `C:\Program Files\Apache Software Foundation\Apache 2.2\htdocs` and locate the `index.php` file.

2. Right-click on this file and choose **Open with | WordPad**.

3. Copy the following lines of code by highlighting the text, right-clicking, and then choosing **Copy**.

4. From **My Computer**, go to `C:\Program Files\Apache Software Foundation\Apache 2.2\htdocs\theme\mytheme`, right-click on the `config.php` file, and choose **Open with | WordPad**.

5. Scroll to the bottom of the file, right-click on a blank line before the closing `?>`, and choose **Paste** to paste the code as set out below, and then save your `config.php` file.

6. Refresh your browser window, and nothing should have changed. Nothing has changed because you are using the same widths as set in the code that you copied and pasted into your `config.php` file.

Continuing with this task, you are simply going to change the width of the left-hand blocks so that you can accommodate an HTML block with some static text in it. You will also look at a couple of blocks that have hardcoded width values, and see what effect these blocks will have on your theme if you use them.

7. Find the following top two lines of code that we have just pasted in:

```
$lmin = (empty($THEME->block_l_min_width)) ? 100 :
$THEME->block_l_min_width;

$lmax = (empty($THEME->block_l_max_width)) ? 210 :
$THEME->block_l_max_width;
```

and change them to:

```
$lmin = (empty($THEME->block_l_min_width)) ? 250 :
$THEME->block_l_min_width;

$lmax = (empty($THEME->block_l_max_width)) ? 250 :
$THEME->block_l_max_width;
```

8. Save your `config.php` file and then refresh your browser. You should notice that your left-hand blocks have become wider.

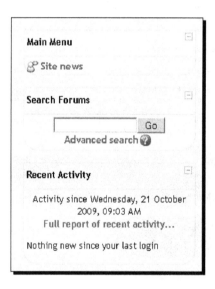

What just happened?

In this exercise, you have re-created what you learned in *Chapter 5, Changing the Layout* by copying the relevant segment of PHP code from the `index.php` file in the root of your Moodle folder and pasting it into the `config.php` file in the root of your theme folder. You then set the left-hand block to be 250px wide both for the minimum setting and for the maximum setting. The left-hand block should remain the same width now, whatever the browser's window size.

You could have set the minimum and maximum left-hand block widths to different values, which would have allowed a small variation in the block's width, depending on the browser window's width or the monitor size. If you wish, you can set these widths to your own values.

Changing the appearance of the blocks

You are now really starting to get your Moodle theme to look like your design mockup, and now need to change the appearance of your blocks to match it. This section will be split into several different tasks, and will require you to "slice and dice" your mockup by using Adobe Photoshop again. You will be adding the gradient header that you created previously to the block headers, and changing the background from a solid color to an image. You will also be changing the border color.

Time for action – creating the block header background

1. Start Adobe Photoshop, and open your design mockup.

2. Hide all of the layers except the block header, by clicking on the eye in the layer's palette for all the layers that you have.

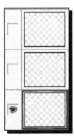

3. Zoom in on the block header by pressing the *Ctrl* and *+* keys together. Zoom in to about 600%.

4. Click on the Rectangular Marquee tool and carefully make a selection from the top to the bottom of the gradient block header.

5. Go to the menu bar and choose **Edit | Copy Merged**. Then select **File | New** and then click on the **OK** button.

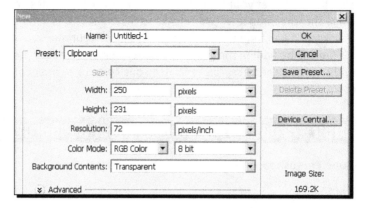

6. Now go to **Edit | Paste**.

7. Then choose menu option **File | Save for Web & Devices**, making sure that your small gradient selection window is in the forefront. Click on **Save**, using the settings below, and name the file `blockheaderback.gif` and save it to the root of your theme directory.

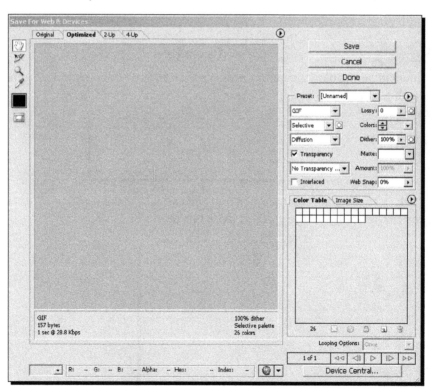

What just happened?

In the last task, you created the gradient background for the block headers of your theme. You took only a very thin slice of the gradient, as you will be using CSS to repeat the strip across the entire width of the block header. This is the technique to use when the width of the element can expand and contract. This way, whatever the width, the background image will repeat itself until the area is filled.

Time for action – changing the block header background

1. Navigate to your Moodle site, and log in as administrator.

2. Open Firebug, and then click on the **Inspect** icon and then hover your mouse over a block header so that the whole header element has a blue highlighted border around it.

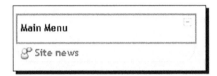

3. Copy the top line of CSS from your right-hand Firebug window, as seen in the following screenshot. This line of CSS controls the sideblock headers.

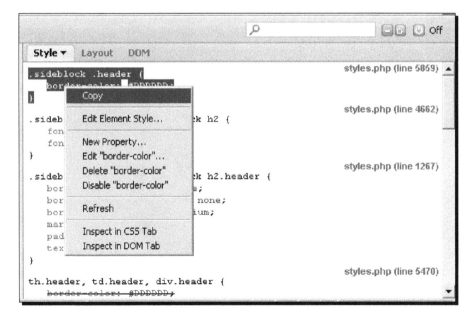

4. Open your `user_styles.css` file, and paste the copied CSS statements into the bottom of the file.

```
.loginbox {
border:1px solid;
margin-bottom:15px;
margin-left:25%;
margin-top:15px;
overflow:hidden;
width:50%;
}

.sideblock .header {
border-color:#DDDDDD;
}
```

5. Change the `.sideblock .header` declaration to:

```
.sideblock .header
{
border-color:#DDDDDD;
-moz-border-radius-topleft:5px;
-moz-border-radius-topright:5px;
background:#E9ECEE url(blockheaderback.gif)
repeat-x scroll center top;
border-width:1px;
min-height:20px;
padding:0px 7px 0px 7px;
}
```

6. Save your `user_styles.css` file, and then refresh your browser window. You now have a nice gradient background for your block headers.

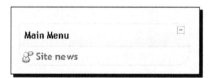

What just happened?

In the last task, you changed your CSS code to load the gradient background that you created in the first exercise. You copied the CSS and pasted it in your `user_styles.css` file, and then made some changes so that the header gradient displays correctly.

One thing to note here is that the following two lines of CSS code work only in Mozilla Firefox, and create a rounded corner on the top right- and left-hand sides of the block header.

```
-moz-border-radius-topleft:5px;
-moz-border-radius-topright:5px;
```

Open Windows Internet Explorer and have a quick look at the block headers. As you can see from the following screenshot, the corners are completely square, but nevertheless actually look fine.

The next line controls the background display properties, and specifically loads the `blockheaderback.gif` and tells the browser to repeat this horizontally across the header.

```
background:#E9ECEE url(blockheaderback.gif) repeat-x scroll center
top;
```

The last three lines set the block's header to have a 1px border and a minimum height of 20px, and give the inside of the block different padding values of `padding-top: 0px`, `padding-right:7px`, `padding-bottom:0px`, and `padding-left:7px`.

```
border-width:1px;
min-height:20px;
padding:0px 7px 0px 7px;
```

Changing the sideblock footer

You now need to change the sideblock footer so that you can reduce the size of the rounded corners on the lower-left and lower-right corners. The footer in this context is actually the content area of the sideblocks, as these do not actually have a footer. Because the *standard* theme has rounded footer corners defined for it, you will need to set these *not* to display rather than setting them to display.

Time for action – reducing the rounded content corners

1. Open your Moodle theme, and using Firebug hover your mouse over one of the block footers. Make sure that you have selected the very outside of it.

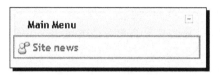

2. Copy the `.sideblock .content` element at the top of the right-hand CSS window.

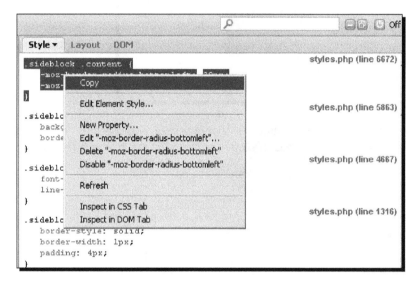

3. Paste this copied code after the `.sideblock .header` element in your `user_styles.css` file.

```
.sideblock .header {
border-color:#DDDDDD;
-moz-border-radius-topleft:5px;
-moz-border-radius-topright:5px;
background:#E9ECEE url(blockheaderback.gif)
border-width:1px;
min-height:20px;
padding:0px 7px 0px 7px;
}

.sideblock .content {
-moz-border-radius-bottomleft:20px;
-moz-border-radius-bottomright:20px;
}
```

4. Change the following lines of CSS code from:

```
-moz-border-radius-bottomleft:20px;
-moz-border-radius-bottomright:20px;
```

to:

```
-moz-border-radius-bottomleft:5px;
-moz-border-radius-bottomright:5px;
```

This reduces the degree to which the lower-left and lower-right corners are rounded.

5. Save the `user_styles.css` file, and then refresh the browser window.

Now your blocks are looking much more like the ones that you created in the graphic mockup created in *Chapter 6*.

What just happened?

In this exercise, you simply copied the `sideblock .content` CSS to your `user_styles.css` file, and changed the `-moz-border-radius` from `20px` to `5px` so as to make the rounded corners a little less pronounced.

Creating the content background

Now that you have reduced the rounded corners on the bottom of the content (footer) on your sideblocks, you can create the gradient background for the sideblock content area. You didn't create one in *Chapter 5, Changing the Layout*, but I think it will make a nice addition to the look of your theme. For this exercise, you will create the background by using Adobe Photoshop again and, once finished, you will change the CSS code to load this background.

Time for action – creating the sideblock content background graphic

1. Open the design mockup in Adobe Photoshop.

2. Make sure that all layers are hidden except for the block border and header as seen below:

3. Zoom in to 200% by pressing the *Ctrl* and *+* keys. Make sure that you can see the whole sideblock.

4. Click on the Rectangular Marquee tool, and then select the inside of the content area of the sideblock.

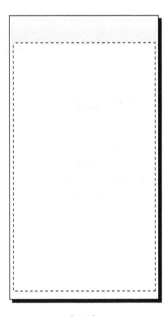

5. Go to the menu bar and choose **Layer | New | New Layer**, and then click on **OK** on the new layer palette.

6. Click on the gradient tool on the tools palette.

The gradient palette should still be set as it was before, but if it isn't, then you will need to make sure that the color chooser has the following colors set:

```
foreground color:#ffffff
background color:#dddddd
```

The gradient palette on the menu bar looks like the example in the following screenshot:

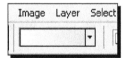

7. Take the cross hair cursor and drag a marquee from the top of your selected layer to the bottom, ensuring that you have a completely vertical line. Let go once you are satisfied with it.

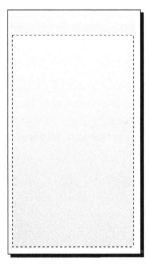

8. Now clear the selection by going to the menu bar and choosing **Select | Deselect**.

9. Click on the Rectangular Marquee tool and draw a selection again from the top to the bottom, but this time only a few pixels wide. You might need to zoom in to do this accurately.

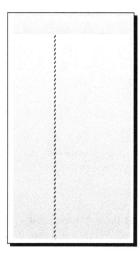

10. Go to the menu bar and select **Edit | Copy Merged**, then select **New | File | OK**, and finally, **Edit | Paste**.

11. Go to **File | Save for Web & Devices,** choose **Save**, and name the file `blockcontentback.gif`. Save this file to the root of your theme's directory.

What just happened?

You just created the gradient background that you are going to use for the background in your block's content area. This process was the same as creating the gradient background for the sideblock header, so you should be getting familiar with this process by now.

You will now change your CSS to load this background and also add some other settings so that it looks correct. One thing to note here is that because you can only load this background gradient horizontally across the page, the gradient part of the background will be visible only to sideblocks of a certain size. Otherwise you will see only the white top part of it.

Also, you have already added a `.sideblock .content` CSS declaration, so you only need to add to this style.

Time for action – changing the block content background

1. Open the `user_styles.css` file, and scroll to the bottom to show the `.sideblock .content` style definition.

```
.sideblock .header {
border-color:#DDDDDD;
-moz-border-radius-topleft:5px;
-moz-border-radius-topright:5px;
background:#E9ECEE url(blockheaderback
border-width:1px;
min-height:20px;
padding:0px 7px 0px 7px;
}

.sideblock .content {
-moz-border-radius-bottomleft:5px;
-moz-border-radius-bottomright:5px;
}
```

2. Add the following line of CSS to the bottom of the `.sideblock .content` class, in order to load the content background.

   ```
   background:#dddddd url(blockcontentback.gif) repeat-x center top;
   ```

   The `repeat-x` element means that the background image is repeated horizontally across the page—which is how the thin slice that we created the background image from fills the whole width of the sideblock.

3. Save the file, and then refresh your browser window.

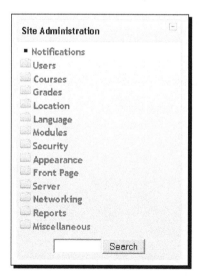

What just happened?

In the last, simple exercise, you changed the CSS code in your `user_styles.css` file to load the gradient background that you created for the content area of the sideblocks. As you can see, some of the smaller sideblocks haven't got this background, for the reason explained earlier. If you can't see the results, make sure that you are logged in as the administrator and are viewing the administration block.

Styling the breadcrumb trail

Sometimes you might find it necessary to style the breadcrumb trail to give it a specific look. The **breadcrumb trail** is the trail of links that take you back one page at a time, and are designed as a navigation aid so that you can navigate up one level easily.

The breadcrumb trail in Moodle is visible only on the inner pages of Moodle, so you will need to click on the **Miscellaneous** course category that is visible on the front page when you are logged in as administrator.

THEME ▶ Course categories ▶ **New Course Category**

As you can see from the preceding screenshot, this doesn't look too bad, and can easily be left alone. However, for the benefit of education, we shall make some small changes to this, by using CSS.

Finding the style used for the breadcrumb trail is a little difficult, as ordinarily it just appears as the normal link style. So first you need to find out what the breadcrumb is called, and the best way of doing this is to change your theme to one that has had its breadcrumb styled.

Time for action – copying a style from another theme

1. Make sure that you are logged into your Moodle site as the administrator, and then navigate to **Appearance | Themes | Theme Selector**, and choose the *Autumn* theme by *Patrick Malley*.

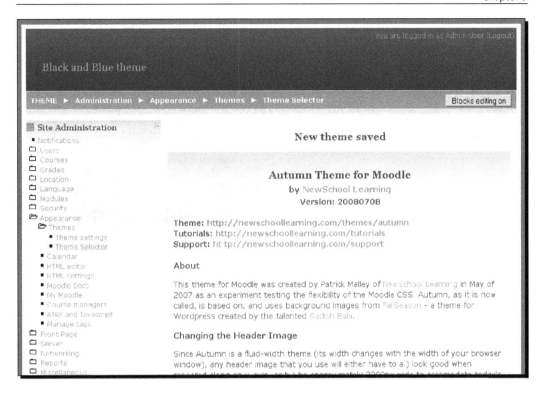

2. Open Firebug, and then hover your mouse over one of the links in the breadcrumb trail, and view the output in the right-hand Firebug window.

3. Copy the top CSS declaration.

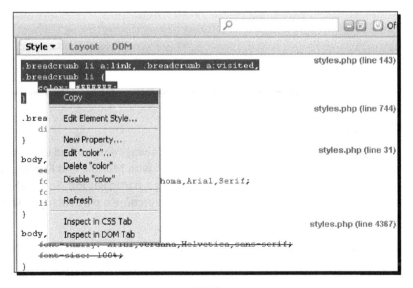

4. Paste this into your `user_styles.css` file, and remove the line:

`color:#FFFFFF;`

Then add the line:

`font-weight:normal;`

5. Save the file, and then reload your *blackandblue* theme. You should notice that the breadcrumb trail now has the normal font weight, and is not bold.

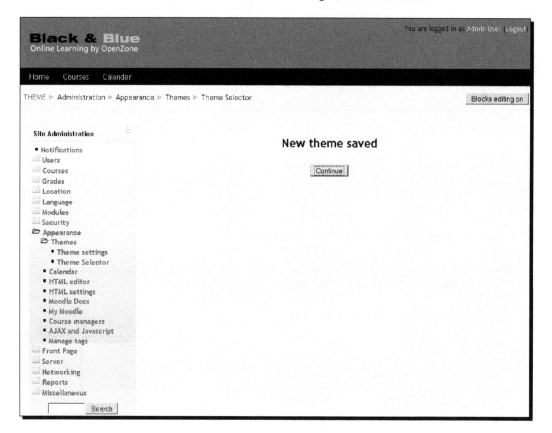

What just happened?

You just learned how to find difficult styles that are not always easy to find even with Firebug. There is always an element of "playing around" with Moodle and Firebug, and sometimes it's not always obvious what styles are doing a particular job. So it's always worth having a look with Firebug at other themes that have overcome a particular problem that you might be having.

Once you have found the CSS style you need, you can copy it and paste it into your own stylesheet.

Have a go hero – correct the padding on the breadcrumb trail

To correct the padding on the breadcrumb trail, you will probably need to create a course and add this course to the miscellaneous category. Once you have done this, click on the **Miscellaneous** category and then on the course that you created. You should notice that the breadcrumb trail is positioned slightly too far from the left-hand side, and doesn't line up with the menu links or the edge of the sideblocks.

Change the padding of the breadcrumb by using CSS, so that it lines up with the other elements on the page.

 Look for the `.navbar` style and use this.

Testing your changes

The final part of this chapter will be to test all of the changes that you have made. I do hope that you have been thinking about this as you worked through the exercises in the chapter. There is nothing worse than working for three hours only to find that the changes that you have made do not work in another browser.

It's also worth pointing out again that all browsers are different and handle HTML and CSS in different ways. So don't be too worried about getting your Moodle theme to look exactly the same in all of the different browsers. Just try to get your theme to look okay in most browsers, and if there are tiny visual differences, don't worry too much.

So now you are going to view your Moodle theme in several different browsers. There will not be any exercises in this section; I will just give you some screenshots and comments about any differences encountered.

Microsoft's Windows Internet Explorer 8.0

The first browser that you are going to test with is Microsoft's Windows Internet Explorer—one of the most popular web browsers available.

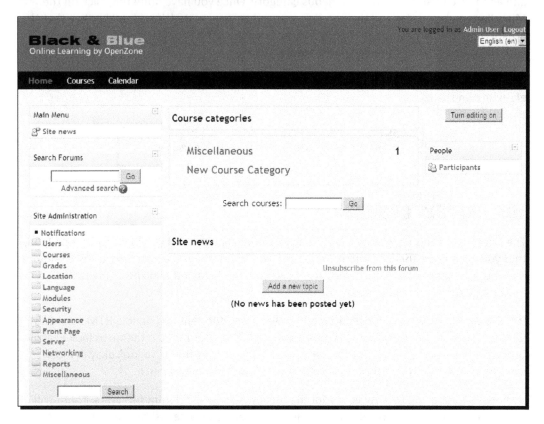

There is nothing untoward in Internet Explorer; everything is in its place. You might notice that the fonts look slightly different, as Internet Explorer smoothens the edges of the screen font. And, as mentioned earlier in this chapter, the CSS for the rounded corners works only in Firefox.

Microsoft's Windows Internet Explorer 7 (8 in compatibility mode)

The next browser is again Windows Internet Explorer, but this time you are using Explorer 7 instead of 8. You can find this by clicking the compatibility icon in the toolbar. This feature just shows you what your theme would look like with Microsoft's previous release of Windows Internet Explorer.

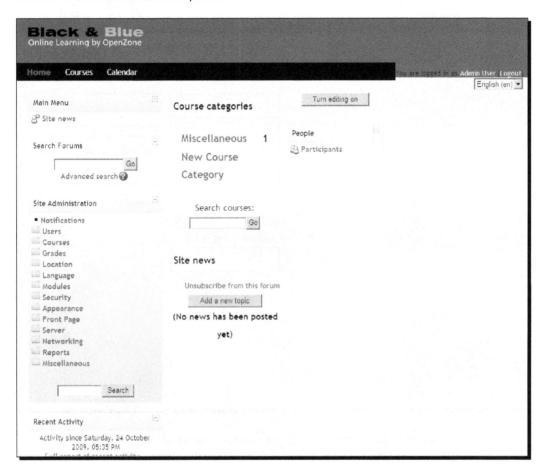

This is not good, as you can see. The header menu with the login info link seems to be causing problems. You will need to fix this, as IE 7 (which is IE 8 in compatibility mode) is currently one of the most used browsers in the world. But for now you will just check this site in other browsers and come back to this problem later.

Apple Safari 4 for Windows

Let's now try Apple Safari for Windows and see what (if any) the differences are.

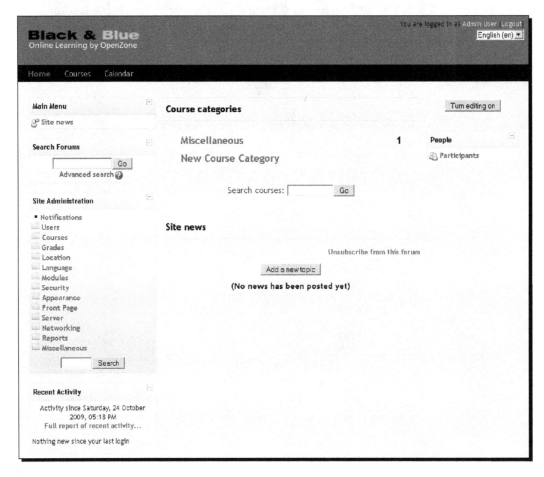

There are problems here. Everything seems to be correct and all of the elements are positioned properly. The only things missing, as before, are the rounded corners.

Google Chrome

Finally, you will check your theme in Google Chrome.

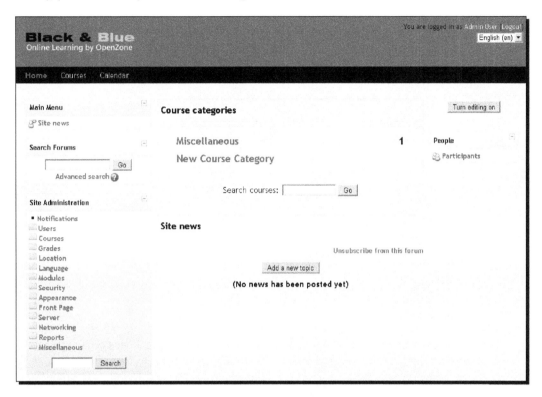

Again, there are no problems with Google Chrome; it looks exactly as expected.

Have a go hero – changing the login info text

If you look carefully at the login info text on the top right-hand corner, you should notice that the text—**You are logged in as**—has a slightly different size than the link text. Make this text the same size.

Look for the .logininfo style.

Have a go hero – fixing the issue in IE 8 (compatibility mode)

Fixing the issue with IE 8 task is slightly more difficult insofar as it relates not only to the CSS code for the .headermenu class that you created for it in your user_styles.css file, but also to the way in which you have created the header.html file.

The reason why the login info text is not positioned properly and is therefore creating issues with your layout is because you haven't grouped your elements properly in your header.html file.

If you feel brave, you could see whether you can fix this issue by correctly grouping the header.html elements. However, there is a quick fix to this, and some tips on how to do this are set out below:

◆ Delete the float:right and padding declarations in the .headermenu style, and replace them with absolute positioning declarations such as:

```
position:absolute
top:10px
right:10px
```

This will move the .headermenu, which contains the login info text and links, to an absolute place on the page, and as such it will no longer interfere with the header and menu areas.

◆ A point to note here is that if you would have checked your changes on a regular basis, you would have spotted the issue with IE 8 (compatibility mode) and would have fixed this before moving on. Also, this issue proves that the other browsers that you have tested in are better at working out what you intended, and in effect automatically worked around some of your mistakes.

Summary

In this chapter, you have learned a lot about creating some of the more advanced elements of your theme. You have learned how to change the appearance of the login screen, and have given a set width to your left-hand sideblocks. You should now also have a better understanding of the steps involved in changing the appearance of your sideblocks, and know how to use graphic files to create better visual effects. You have also learned how to find missing styles by copying these from other themes, should you not be able to find them in the *standard* theme.

Specifically, we covered:

- Changing the appearance of the login screen
- Setting the width of our sideblocks
- Using a gradient graphic for our block headers and content areas
- Styling the breadcrumb trail
- Understanding the importance of browser compatibility and checking that our changes have worked

In the next chapter, you will be working on some of the more advanced theming techniques, and will be concentrating on changing the appearance of your course view so that it matches the rest of your theme. You will then move on to theming some of the core modules so that your theme looks consistent throughout the user experience. The modules that you will be theming are the forums, blog, glossary, quiz, and wiki.

10
Under the Hood: Theming Core Functionality and Modules

In Chapter 10, you will be changing the appearance of some of the core code (non-contributed) parts of Moodle. You will first look at theming the central content part of your Moodle site, including the home page course category pages and the actual course view. You will move on to learn how to theme the forum and glossary modules to match your theme. You will be changing only a small amount in each module so that you can pave the way for further improvements in Chapter 11.

Theming the central area of our Moodle site

It is true to say that one of the issues with theming Moodle is that you cannot edit the central content section of your site, as it does not have an associated HTML file. The only areas that you can really edit are the header and footer. However, you can nevertheless use CSS to make some changes to the way the central section looks. You can change fonts, font colors and sizes, and add borders and backgrounds to the central page elements. You can therefore get away with making these areas at least look reasonable in terms of matching your existing theme's look and feel. You cannot, however, move any of the central content elements, such as the login info link or the placement of your logo, as you can in the header and footer. You also cannot add anything to this section in terms of HTML or PHP elements or functionality without changing the core code. And you do not really want to change the core code because when you come to update your Moodle installation to a new release, your changes will be overwritten if you have not carefully logged the changes down in a changelog or created a patch file.

Set out below are the two most important central areas of your Moodle site—namely the home page **course categories** and the **course view** elements.

Home page: Course categories area:

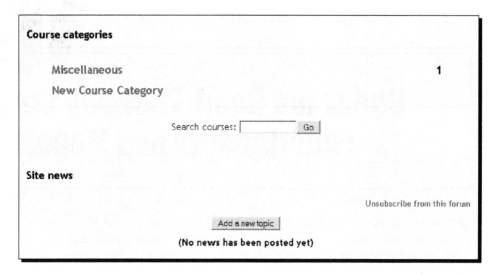

Course view:

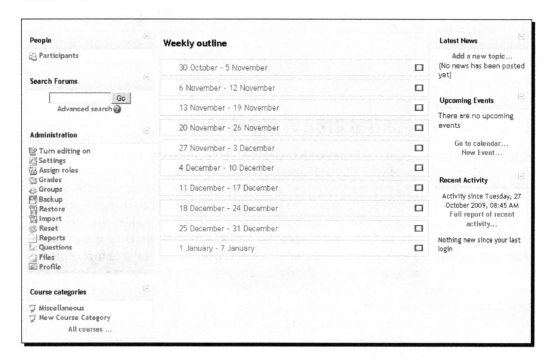

Adding a course category and a sample course

If you are using a fresh installation of Moodle and you log in as the administrator, you will notice that you do not have any courses and that you have only one **Miscellaneous** category. If this is the case, you will first need to add another course category and a sample course, so that you can get on with theming these functional elements of your Moodle site. Of course, there is a likelihood that you have already done this or that you have courses already in use, in which case you can skip over the next task.

Time for action – adding a new course category and course to Moodle

1. Navigate to your Moodle site, log in as the administrator and make sure you are on the front page of your site, which is `http://yourmoodle.com` if you are using your organization's current Moodle VLE, or `http://localhost` if you have set Moodle up locally on your own computer.

2. In the **Site Administration** block, navigate to **Courses | Add/edit courses**. You can see that I have already added a new category but I will delete it for this exercise.

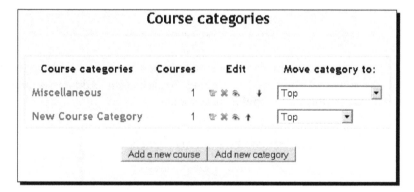

3. Click on the **Add new category** button on the bottom right-hand side.

4. Fill in the following details in the **Add new category** page, and then click on the **Create category** button.

5. The new page will give you the opportunity to add a course and assign this course to the category that you have just created. So click on the **Add a new course** button in the middle of this rather confusing screen.

6. Fill in the **Edit course settings** page with the following details. Ignore any fields that are not shown in the following image, and click on the **Save changes** button at the very bottom of the screen.

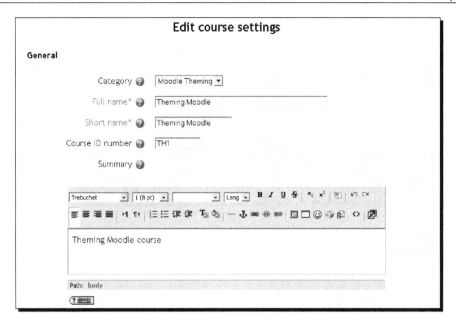

7. Ignore the next screen, and click on the **Click here to enter your course** button.

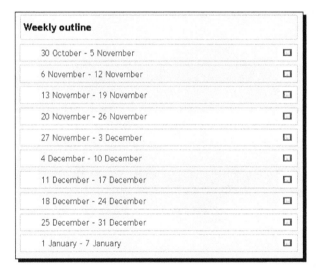

What just happened?

In the last simple task, you learned how to create a new course category and add a course to this category. This needed to be done so that you now have some extra details on the home page **course categories** central area, and you have an actual course to start to theme.

Further information can be found in the Moodle docs at:
`http://docs.moodle.org/en/Courses_(administrator)`.

Theming the course category section

In this section, you are going to start to theme the course category section. This isn't totally necessary, but is worth it as you can make the course category headers match those of your block headers in order to give your theme a consistent look and feel.

Time for action – changing the background color

1. Click the word `theme` on your breadcrumb trail to take you back to the front page.

2. Open Firebug and click on the **Inspect** icon, and then hover your mouse over the **Course categories** box at the top of your Moodle site.

Course categories	
Miscellaneous	2
Moodle Theming	1

Search courses: [   ] [Go]

Site news

3. Inspect the CSS output in the right-hand Firebug window.

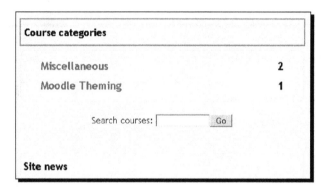

The top line of CSS in the previous screenshot adds a margin of 9px to the `body#site-index`, the `.heading` block class, and the `course-view` heading block. Change is wanted only in the background of the **Course category** area, so you should leave the top class as it is. The second class only alters the font size of the text in the heading blocks, so you will also leave this for now. The third style is the one that we are after, which will change the background to all of the heading blocks. This is good, as it will create a consistent look throughout your theme.

4. Copy the third style and paste this into the `user_styles.css` file, as seen in the next two screenshots:

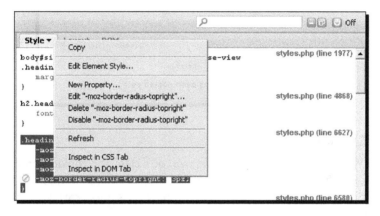

5. Add the following style to the bottom of the `.headingblock` class, and then save your `user_styles.css` file.

    ```
    background-color: #faf9fa;
    ```

6. Refresh your browser window.

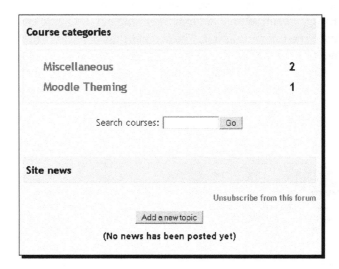

What just happened?

In this exercise, you simply found the `.headingblock` class and copied it to your `user_styles.css` file. You then made a small change to adjust the color of the background and subsequently changed the background of not only the **Course categories** header block but also the **Site news** heading block.

This is by design, and is what we wanted.

The `.headingblock` class comes from the standard theme's `styles_layout.css` file and is overwritten once you copy and paste it into your `user_styles.css` file.

Time for action – changing the header fonts

1. Go back to your browser and make sure that your Moodle site is visible.

2. Open Firebug again, click on the **Inspect** icon, and then hover your mouse over the **Course categories** area as you did in the last task. You should see the same output in the right-hand Firebug window as before.

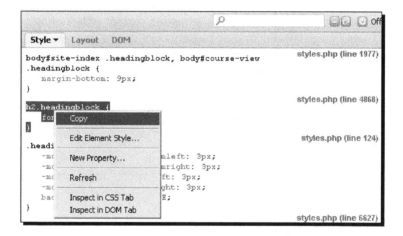

3. Copy the second style and paste this into your `user_styles.css` file.

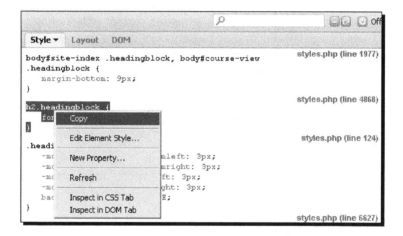

4. Change the following line:

   `font-size:1.1em;`

   to:

   `font-size:1.0em;`

> The pixel measurement em is a relative font-size and is dependent on the size that the font is set to by the parent element and by the user's browser. 1.0 em is equal to the current font size.

5. Save your `user_styles.css` file and refresh your browser window.

> **Course categories**

What just happened?

You have just reduced the font-size in the **Course categories** and **Site news** headers by a small amount. If you wish, you can experiment and try to change the color of the font used in the `.headingblock` class as well.

Theming the course view

One of the most important tasks that any budding Moodle themer has to do is to theme the course view in Moodle, as this is the place that is visited the most (apart from the front page). This section can be left alone if you think that the current style is good enough. By "good enough" I mean that the course view section's font can be read easily and clearly, and there is suitable balance in terms of contrast between the background and foreground. However, on most occasions, a Moodle themer will want to make sure that the course view matches the rest of the theme that they are building.

Have a quick look at the course view and see what you think. Navigate to the home page and click on the **Moodle theming** category and then on the theming Moodle course that you created earlier.

Weekly outline	
30 October - 5 November	☐
6 November - 12 November	☐
13 November - 19 November	☐
20 November - 26 November	☐
27 November - 3 December	☐
4 December - 10 December	☐
11 December - 17 December	☐
18 December - 24 December	☐
25 December - 31 December	☐
1 January - 7 January	☐

Now some people would say that this looks alright and should be left as it is, but as we are perfectionists, we shall be making some changes to it. My first comment is that the font color used for the weeks in each of the weekly topic areas is a little light in color and could be made darker so that the user can see it more clearly.

You could also add a slightly darker background to each of the topic sections so that they also stand out a little better.

Finally, you could change the icons used to show and hide the rest of the topics as seen on the right-hand side of each topic section.

Time for action – changing the font color

1. Open your Moodle site and Firebug, navigate to the **Theming Moodle** course that you created, and then hover your mouse over one of the weekly topic sections, making sure that you get the very inner area around the date.

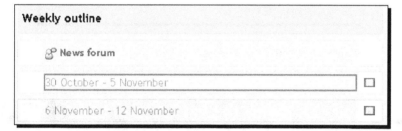

2. View the output in the right-hand Firebug window.

3. Copy the top class and paste this into your `user_styles.css` file, and then save your changes.

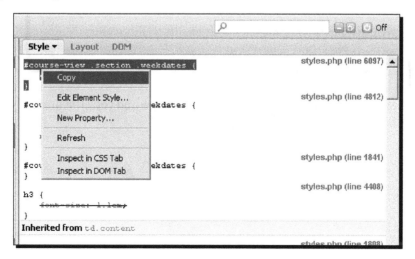

4. Change the following CSS code from:

```
#course-view .section .weekdates {
color:#777777;
}
```

To:

```
#course-view .section .weekdates {
color:#000000;
}
```

5. Save the `user_styles.css` file and refresh your browser window.

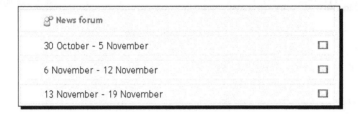

As you can see, we have changed the dates from a light gray color to black, and now they are a little more visible. Next we will make the background a little darker.

Time for action – changing the background color

1. Open Firebug and inspect the whole middle section of one of the topic areas.

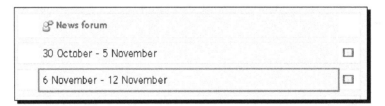

2. View the output in the right-hand Firebug window and copy the first class. Then paste this into your `user_styles.css` file.

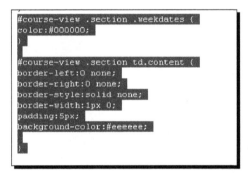

3. Add the following CSS code to the bottom of the style that you have just pasted into your `user_styles.css` file:

```
background-color:#eeeeee;
```

Your `user_styles.css` file should now look like the following screenshot:

4. Save this file, and then refresh your browser window.

The last task that you are going to perform on the course view section is simply to replace the blue **Hide** and **Show** icons on the right-hand side for something that looks a little better. If you right-click on the image and select **Properties** from the dialog box that appears, you can easily find out what the image is called and where it is stored.

The hard part of this task is to find two suitable icons for the job. I like the ones in the *Foodle* theme, so it would be a good idea at this stage for you to go to the main `moodle.org` website and download the *Foodle* theme and install it. We will not be going through this step by step, as you should know how to do this by now.

 Always check that the icons that you use have a license that allows their reproduction or use in other Moodle themes.

So please go ahead and download the *Foodle* theme and install it. Once you have done this, you can then set Moodle to use this theme so that you can have a look at the icons.

Foodle course view:

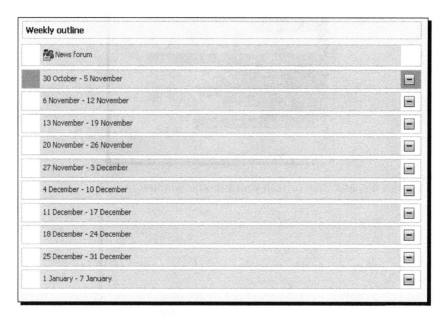

Time for action – copying the show/hide icons

1. Right-click on the **Hide** icon, as visible in the image above, and choose **Save image as** and then click **Save**. This should save the icon to the same directory in your `blackandblue` theme folder. Make sure that this is the case before clicking the **Save** button.

2. When the overwrite dialog box appears, choose **Yes**.

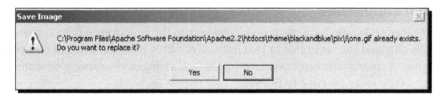

3. Go back to the *Foodle* course and click on the icon that you have just saved, to collapse all of the weeks in the course and display the **Show** icon.

4. Right-click on this icon and choose **Save image as** again, and then choose **Yes** in response to the overwrite warning.

5. Navigate back to the home page and then change the theme from *Foodle* back to your *blackandblue* theme.

6. Navigate to the **Theming Moodle** course and then press *Ctrl + F5*. This will clear the cache from your browser and load the new icons.

What just happened?

In the last three tasks, you have made some changes to the course view in your theme. You successfully changed the font color so that it displays a little more clearly, and also changed the background color of the topic sections. Finally, you changed the show/hide icons to something a little more pleasing to the eye.

If icons for your current theme are copied into your theme's `mytheme\pix` folder, Moodle will automatically load these in place of the icons normally loaded from the `htdocs\pix` folder. So if no icons are present in your `mytheme\pix` folder, Moodle will look in the `htdocs\pix` folder for the default icons.

Changing the appearance of the core modules

This part of the chapter will focus on changing the appearance of some of the core modules so that they will blend in nicely with the theme that we are building. We will not be changing all of the core activity modules because some will be left to change on your own at the end of this book. The modules that we will be changing are the forum and glossary modules.

Forum module

The first—and probably the most important—module to change is the **forum module**. This module is used extensively through Moodle, and is added by default to every course created. It is also the module that is used for the site news on the home page of Moodle. You will not be making huge changes here, but will just be changing the border and the header so that they look like the block headers that you created earlier. Again, you can do what you like here, so if you want to change a particular element, or wish to have a different color font than we have, please go ahead and do so.

Time for action – changing the forum summary box

1. Open your Moodle site and log in as the administrator.

2. Navigate to the **Moodle Theming** category and then to the **Theming Moodle** course.

3. Click on the **News forum** at the top of the course, to enter that forum.

4. Open Firebug and click on the **Inspect** icon, and then hover your mouse over the summary box as seen below:

5. View the Firebug output in the right-hand window, and then copy the two top styles, one at a time.

6. Paste these into the bottom of your `user_styles.css` file.

7. Change the `width` from `70%` to `90%`, and add a background color of #eeeeee, as seen below:

```
#course-view .section td.content {
border-left:0 none;
border-right:0 none;
border-style:solid none;
border-width:1px 0;
padding:5px;
background-color:#eeeeee;

}

#intro.generalbox {
margin-left:auto;
margin-right:auto;
padding-bottom:15px;
width:90%;
background-color:#eeeeee;
}
```

8. Save your `user_styles.css` file, and then refresh your browser window. The summary box should have become a little wider, and the background should have changed to a shade of gray, as shown below:

General news and announcements

9. Now change the `.generalbox` and reduce the corner width to `3px` and add a gradient background as well.

```
#intro.generalbox {
margin-left:auto;
margin-right:auto;
padding-bottom:15px;
width:90%;
background-color:#eeeeee;
}

.generalbox {
-moz-border-radius-bottomleft:3px;
-moz-border-radius-bottomright:3px;
-moz-border-radius-topleft:3px;
-moz-border-radius-topright:3px;
background:url(blockheaderback.gif) repeat-x scroll center top;

}
```

10. Refresh your browser window, and your summary box now has more subtle corners and has a nice gradient background.

General news and announcements

One thing to note here is that the `#.generalbox` style applies to all of the general boxes throughout your site, so you have effectively removed the large rounded corners and added a gradient background to all of the boxes on your Moodle site. This is the case for many of Moodle's CSS styles, so I recommend that when you change styles that have a generic name, such as `.generalbox`, check over your entire site, in a variety of browsers, in case of unexpected display problems. Let's move swiftly onto customizing the display of the discussions and posts of the forum module.

Time for action – customizing the forum

1. Open Firebug and hover your mouse over the **Discussion** box as seen below:

Discussion

Moodle theme forum

2. Copy the top CSS class from the Firebug window, and paste it into the bottom of your `user_styles.css` file.

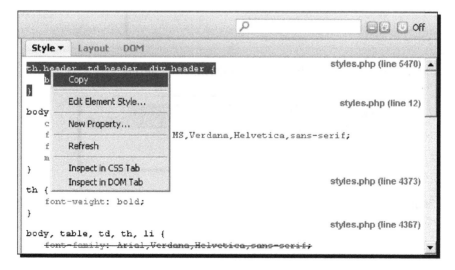

3. Change this CSS statement so that the class looks like the one below:

```
.generalbox {
-moz-border-radius-bottomleft:3px;
-moz-border-radius-bottomright:3px;
-moz-border-radius-topleft:3px;
-moz-border-radius-topright:3px;
}

th.header {
background-color:#FFFFFF;
background:url(blockheaderback.gif) repeat-x scroll center top;
}
```

4. Save and refresh your browser window.

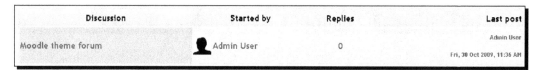

5. Now click on the **Inspect** icon in Firebug and hover your mouse over the forum name, and then copy the top class from your Firebug window. Paste this copied class into your `user_styles.css` file.

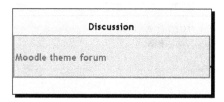

6. Change the CSS code to look like the following screenshot:

```
.forumheaderlist .discussion .starter {
background:transparent none repeat scroll 0 0;
border-right:#eeeeee 1px solid;
padding-left:10px;
}
```

7. Repeat this for the `lastpost` forum header and the `lastpost` content area below it, and change the two classes to look like the next screenshot:

```
.forumheaderlist .discussion .lastpost {
font-size:0.7em;
padding-right:10px;
}

.forumheaderlist .lastpost {
text-align:right;
white-space:nowrap;
padding-right:10px;
}
```

8. Save the file, and then refresh your browser.

Discussion	Started by	Replies	Last post
Moodle theme forum	Admin User	0	Admin User Fri, 30 Oct 2009, 11:36 AM

What just happened?

In the last exercise, you changed several parts of the forum module. You have added the same gradient background to the forum header that you used for the block headers. You also changed the background color of the forum name area from gray to white, and gave both the last post header and the content area a padding value to move the text away from the edge. Finally, you made the text slightly smaller.

You now need to change the appearance of the actual forum post. This can be seen either in the forum that you are currently editing or in the front page news section. Changing the width of the forum post is a little trickier, but the solution has been added to the Moodle documentation.

Time for action – customizing the forum posts

1. Navigate to the **Theming Moodle** category and then to the **Theming Moodle** course. Click on the news forum at the top. You should now be in the forum that you have just changed.

2. Click on the **Moodle theme forum** thread to show the actual forum post.

3. Add the following code to the end of the `user_styles.css` file, and then save your changes.

```
.mod-forum #content {
    text-align: left;
}
.mod-forum #content .forumpost {
    width: 95%; /*or 65%;*/
    text-align: left;
    margin: 10px auto 0;
}
.mod-forum #content .indent {
    width: 95%; /*65%;*/
    text-align: left;
    margin-left: 4%;
    margin-right: auto;
}
.mod-forum #content .forumthread {
    width: 95%; /*65%;*/
    text-align: left;
    padding-left: 8%;
}
#mod-forum-post #content .generalboxcontent {
    text-align: left;
}
```

4. Refresh your browser window. The forum post should now extend across the full width of the page.

5. Now add the following CSS to the `user_styles.css` file, and save your changes again.

```
.forumpost .starter {
    background:url(blockheaderback.gif) repeat-x scroll center top;
}
```

6. Refresh your browser window—the first forum in the list now has a gradient background for its header.

7. Finally, add the following three styles to the `user_styles.css` file, to reduce the rounded corners on the forum posts.

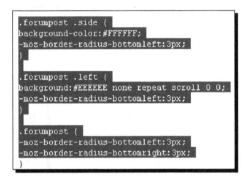

```
.forumpost .side {
background-color:#FFFFFF;
-moz-border-radius-bottomleft:3px;
}

.forumpost .left {
background:#EEEEEE none repeat scroll 0 0;
-moz-border-radius-bottomleft:3px;
}

.forumpost {
-moz-border-radius-bottomleft:3px;
-moz-border-radius-bottomright:3px;
}
```

8. Save the file, and then refresh your browser window.

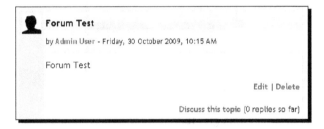

What just happened?

In the last, simple task, you changed the forum post header to include the same gradient background that you used for your theme sideblocks. You also changed the forum post so that it spans 95% of the screen width, and reduced the amount of curvature on the corners of the forum posts.

Glossary module

The next module that you are going to change is the **glossary module**. This module is normally used quite a lot by educators and is therefore another module that you might want to change. If you need to know what activity modules are the most popular on your site, you can navigate to `http://yourmoodlesite/admin/modules.php`. Here you will find a list of all of the activity modules, and how many instances of that module are present on your Moodle site. However, this option really works only for sites that are already being used. Consequently, this method will not give you much information if you have a `localhost` install of Moodle. You shall be making the corners have the same curvature as the forum posts in an effort to make everything a little more consistent. But before you start, you need to quickly create a glossary so that you can edit its CSS code.

Time for action – creating a glossary

1. Log in as an administrator, and navigate to the **Theming Moodle** course.

2. Click on the **Turn editing on** button, to add resources and activities to the Moodle course.

3. Click on the **Add an activity** drop-down box and choose **Glossary**.

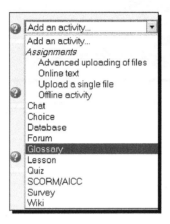

4. Name the glossary **Moodle glossary** and add the same text to the description field, and then click on the **Save and display** button at the bottom of the screen.

5. Click the **Add new entry** button at the top of the page, and enter some sample text.

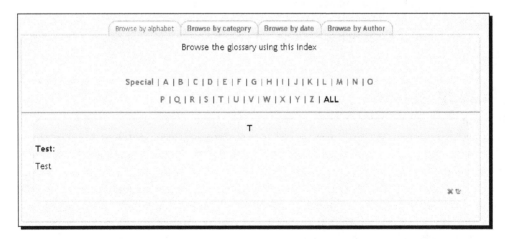

Now that you have a sample glossary, you can move on and reduce the size of the corners of the central glossary entry area. More information about using the Glossary module can be found at: `http://docs.moodle.org/en/Glossary`.

Time for action – customizing the glossary resource

1. Open your `user_styles.css` file, and enter the following code into it, just as you did with the forum post:

```
.glossarypost {
-moz-border-radius-bottomleft:3px;
-moz-border-radius-bottomright:3px;
}
```

2. Save this file, and then refresh your browser window. You have just made the bottom corners of the glossary post less rounded, just as you did with the forum post exercise.

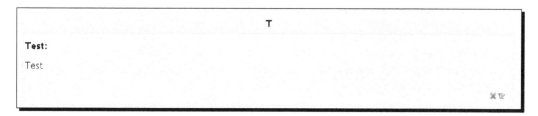

3. Now open the `user_styles.css` file again, and enter the following CSS code. Save the file, and then refresh your browser.

```
.glossarycategoryheader {
    -moz-border-radius-topleft:3px;
    -moz-border-radius-topright:3px;
}
```

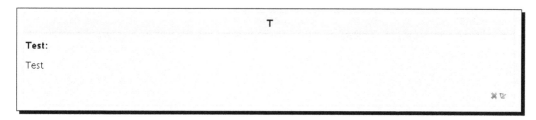

A tip to consider is that if you can't find the correct styles by using Firebug, you can go to the *standard* theme's folder and find the styles for that particular module or glossary, and copy them all. You can then paste them into your user_styles.css file and slowly make changes to each individual style until you see the area that you are working on change. In this way, you can identify the correct styles for any given element on your Moodle site.

Have a go hero – adding a gradient background to all posts

When you added a gradient header to the forum posts, you only changed the first post or the forum post starter. Go back to this, and change the header to include a gradient for all posts. You will need to reply to the test post so that you can see any changes that you make.

Summary

In this chapter, you have delved under the hood and learned how to theme the look and feel of the front page courses category section and the actual Moodle courses. You have learned how to change the fonts, colors, and backgrounds of the courses, and have learned how to change the show/hide icons on the right-hand side of the topic sections. You have also learned how to theme the forums and forum posts, and continued with this by changing the appearance of the glossary pages and glossary posts.

Specifically, we covered:

- Changing the background and fonts used in the course category section
- Theming the course view font colors, headers, and backgrounds
- Changing the appearance of the forum summary box
- Changing the appearance of the forums and the forum posts
- Creating a glossary resource and customizing its look and feel

In the next chapter, we will look at some further enhancements that we can make to our theme. There will not be any exercises in that chapter—we will just discuss some more changes that we can make to improve our theme. We will also look at some best practices, and look at how we can deal with any theming issues that we might encounter when theming a Moodle site.

We will also check our theme against as many browsers as we can, and look at running some validators over our Moodle site in order to check it against the current HTML and accessibility standards.

Further Enhancements

In this appendix, we will discuss some further enhancements that you can make to your newly created theme. Obviously, we have missed various small changes that could be implemented while working through these chapters, so we will concentrate on those. We will also discuss ways by which you can streamline some of the actions that you have been undertaking. For instance, you can group CSS styles so that one can be applied to many instances throughout your theme. At this stage, you can also download the Moodle features demo course, so that you can check that your theme works with all of the standard Moodle features such as assignments, chats, choices, databases, lessons, and quizzes. You will also correct a few problems that the author has noticed. You will also look at how to create rollover and drop-down menus, amongst other things.

Some further small changes

As we have progressed through the chapters of this book, there are a few small changes that we could have made as we worked through them. We didn't make these changes because it would have made some of the chapters a little long, and I felt that it would be best if you (the reader) tried to change these with only a few small hints and tips.

Try to make the following changes by using some of the hints set out below.

Changing the buttons

One thing that I thought might need to be changed was the look and feel of the button elements in your theme. You can change the color, size, and font, or even implement a rollover so that the button changes color when the user places his or her mouse over the button. Set out below is an example of two buttons—one styled using CSS and in the active state and the other in a rollover state.

Active state:

Turn editing on

Rollover state:

Turn editing on

Let's see if you can make the form buttons in your theme look like the ones above. Remember: you can add backgrounds, borders, change the font type and size, and even have a rollover state for the buttons.

Here is a CSS hint:

```
input[type="button"], input[type="submit"]
button:hover, input[type="button"]:hover, input[type="submit"]:hover
```

Changing the drop-down fields

Another thing that you might want to sort out is the drop-down fields, such as the language chooser on the top right-hand corner of your theme. These can be styled, but not as much as the buttons. Another thing to look out for is that elements often share classes, so changing the width of one might have an effect on another.

So go and jump in and see if you can find the correct class that will alter the look of the language drop-down box on your theme, by using Firebug.

It's not there, is it? Well here is a tip: look in the *standard* theme's stylesheets for a style called **select**. Here is an example of a drop-down form field that has been styled:

English (en)

Changing the form fields

Again, there are lots of form fields scattered around Moodle, and there is no reason why you shouldn't make these look a little better as well.

```
button, input[type="password"], input[type="text"]
```

The above CSS hint might help you with this, but make sure that the correct form fields are changed. Here is an example of a form text field that has been styled:

Rollover menu

Another improvement that can be made is to create a better rollover effect when the user hovers his or her mouse over any of the menu links. For instance, you can highlight the whole background rather than just the actual link. Below is an example of what can be achieved with this technique. Again, this is done entirely through the use of CSS.

Creating a rollover menu

To create this effect, it is normally a simple matter of adding a background to the `.hover` class in your `user_styles.css` file. But remember: because these links have a different style than the rest of the links in your theme, you need to apply this background hover style to the `#menu` class.

However, in this case, it is a little more complex, so I will outline the changes to the code. You will need to replace the CSS of all the `#menu` links with the CSS set out below:

```
#menu a:link, a:active, a:visted
{
  font-weight:normal;
  color:#ffffff;
  text-decoration:none;
  font-size:92%;
}
#menu   {
padding-left:20px;

}

#menu a {
padding-left:10px;
padding-right:10px;
padding-top:5px;
padding-bottom:5px;
 font-weight:normal;
 color:#ffffff;
}

#menu a:hover
{
  color:#000000;
  background:#a1b2f0;
  text-decoration:none;
  font-weight:normal;
}
```

You will then need to remove the menu spacers in your `menu.php` file. These are `  ::  ` and are at the end of the `a href` link code.

You menu should now look like the following screenshot:

Creating a drop-down menu

When your Moodle theme and site is finished, you will probably find that more and more support organizations around your college or university will want a presence on Moodle. These can range from a library link to student support, employability, and so on. If this happens, you might find that there isn't enough room on your horizontal menu for all of these links. A way around this is to create categories and have a drop-down menu so that you can fit more links into the menu.

Have a look at the *Newbury College* theme on the main Moodle site as an example of this. They have created a nice, and sleek drop-down menu that works in most available web browsers. There are many resources where you can find the drop-down menu code—one such place is `http://www.cssmenu.co.uk`.

If you choose to use a drop-down menu that you have found on the Internet, please ensure that you test that it works in as many browsers as you can find.

Just choose the menu dropdown of your choice, and download the ZIP file. Once you have done that, copy the CSS from the CSS file, paste it in to your `user_styles.css` file, and save your changes. Do the same for the HTML file, but remember to add this code to the `menu.php` file.

It would be prudent to suggest that you should comment out the `#menu` link code that you added in the last task, so that if you have problems you can revert to it. The same goes for the `menu.php` and the HTML code that you added to it.

There will be an amount of CSS customization to complete, but it's a matter of experiment and poking around with the CSS that you have downloaded.

Consolidating your CSS code

There are times when CSS files become very large and unwieldy because you have copied or created a lot of styles. In this case, and for the sake of keeping your styles nicely organized, you can tidy them up a little and consolidate them to make the whole file a little more organized.

Grouping styles

Often, styles created through CSS can be grouped into one class, so that one style can affect many elements on the page. Assume that you want an image header for your block headers and your general boxes throughout your theme. In previous examples, you have simply copied the `sideblock` header class and applied a background to this style, as seen below:

```
.sideblock .header {
border-color:#DDDDDD;
-moz-border-radius-topleft:5px;
-moz-border-radius-topright:5px;
background:#E9ECEE url(blockheaderback.gif) repeat-x;
border-width:1px;
min-height:20px;
padding:0px 7px 0px 7px;
}
```

You then copied the `.generalbox` style, and gave that a background, as shown:

```
.generalbox {
-moz-border-radius-bottomleft:3px;
-moz-border-radius-bottomright:3px;
-moz-border-radius-topleft:3px;
-moz-border-radius-topright:3px;
background:url(blockheaderback.gif) repeat-x scroll center top;
}
```

If these CSS classes had exactly the same requirements—that is, they only required the background and nothing else—then they could have been grouped as shown below:

```
.sideblock .header, .generalbox {
background:#E9ECEE url(blockheaderback.gif) repeat-x;
}
```

This technique is normally employed when the element needs only simple CSS applied to it. For instance, if you just wanted the background of a lot of elements to have a gray color, then this technique could be employed.

Creating CSS shorthand

Another way of consolidating CSS code, and therefore tidying it up and making the file smaller, is to create your CSS by using a kind of shorthand. Have a look at the following code snippet:

```
.menu {
font-color: #000000;
font-family: verdana, tahoma, helvetica;
font-weight:bold;
}
```

This can be written as:

```
.menu {
font-color: #000000 verdana, tahoma, helvetica bold;
}
```

This means that your CSS file can be made a lot smaller and look a lot tidier. Go and see if you can reduce the amount of CSS in your user_styles.css file, and also see if you can group your styles, and comment the different groups, such as menu, header, and so on.

Correcting some problems

As you have been building your theme, I have noticed a few problems that will need to be sorted out. These have been intentionally left out as a way of getting you (the reader) to try to fix these issues without having the help of guided exercises.

Fixing the .generalbox problem

The first problem that you may have noticed is that in an earlier task you added a gradient background to the .generalbox class to make it look like your sideblocks. This change has created a problem insofar as some of the "generalbox" page elements have text that overlaps the background.

This is because the background gradient that you used is the same as the one used for your sideblocks and is only 32px high. In general, this effect works quite well, but there are other techniques that you could employ to achieve the desired result. You could, for instance, move any overlapping content by giving the .generalbox class a top-padding value. Or better still, you could create a larger (higher) gradient image specifically for the generalbox elements. Give it a go, and try to see if you can come up with an alternative method of sorting out this problem.

Downloading the Moodle features demo

One of the best ways to test your theme is to download and install the Moodle features demo course. This course has been built specifically to display and demonstrate all of the different features that Moodle has to offer, and therefore can be used as a tool to test your theme in every possible circumstance.

Installing the Moodle features demo

Connect to the Internet and navigate to `Moodle.org`, and then browse to
About | Demonstration site (in the top menu).

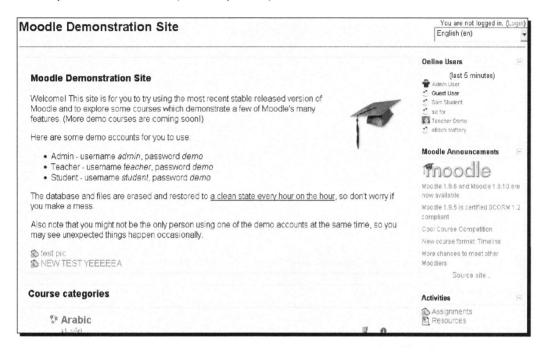

Once you are in the Moodle demonstration site, scroll down to the **English** category, and click on the **Moodle Features Demo** link. This will take you to the Moodle features demo course. Moodle might ask you to log in and if it does, then log in as "admin" with the password as "demo". You will then be taken to the Moodle features demo page, and in the top left-hand sideblock, there will be a link to download the Moodle features demo course. If you cannot see this block, then it could have been deleted by other users. The Moodle features demo course is reset every hour on the hour, so if it's not there, you might have to try again after an hour.

Download this demo to your desktop or somewhere that you know where it is. Now go back to the Moodle site and create a new course, and then restore the Moodle features demo to this course. I am assuming that you know how to do this, but if you don't, there are plenty of tutorials and documentation on `Moodle.org`.

As you can see from the previous screenshot (not the whole course), all of the Moodle features are present here.

Testing all of the features with our new theme

Now that you have the Moodle features demo course installed, you can use this to test all of the features of your theme. This is a great way to test, as there is nearly always something that goes wrong in the theming process that could be overlooked if you don't check every feature thoroughly in all of the most popular browsers.

So go ahead and open Internet Explorer, Firefox, Google Chrome, and Apple Safari for Windows and test each feature, one at a time, in all these four web browsers. You are not testing functionality here, just your theme and how it looks for all of the Moodle features.

Creating a separate course theme

The next advanced feature that you could build into Moodle is creating a separate course theme.

Why would we do this?

Sometimes, educators might want a completely different look and feel for their courses, or require a special course theme for accessibility issues. They might, for instance, be teaching students specifically with visual disabilities, in which case a specific course theme would need to be built. Another scenario where a course theme could be implemented would be for testing. It is perfectly normal for some theme designers to build their theme inside a course to test the features before implementing it globally across their whole Moodle site.

If you can remember back as far as *Chapter 2, Moodle Themes*, you will know that Moodle themes have a priority, and are applied hierarchically in this order:

Site > User > Session > Category > Course > Page.

How do we do this?

To create a course theme, you would just need to create a dummy course, maybe with the Moodle features demo course material added to it, and set **Allow course themes** in the **Theme settings** page in the administration block. Then just go to the settings for that course and choose the theme that you are working on.

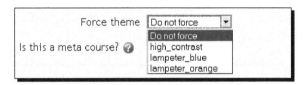

You could call this theme something like "Do not use" so that educators do not choose it while you are working on it.

Checking our theme against W3C validators

Another useful thing to do is to check that what you have created passes some of the more important guidelines of **World Wide Web Consortium (W3C)**. These have been set up so that web designers/developers create consistent code for their sites and that websites are accessible to all. In general, there are two different validators that you can use; these are HTML validators and accessibility validators.

HTML validators simply check your code against what has been decided upon as the correct way of coding HTML. With Moodle, you get to change only the `header.html` and `footer.html` files, so these are the only pages that will need to be checked.

Accessibility validators check that websites are accessible to people with disabilities, and therefore are important if your Moodle site is in the public domain.

 Remember, these validators will only work on publicly-accessible domains and will not work on a localhost installation of Moodle.

What validators do we check against?

The best way to test for accessibility is to check your theme against the **Web Content Accessibility Guidelines (WCAG)**, but don't leave out the option of having disabled users actually test the site for you. In this circumstance, you could have valuable evidence if any legal issues arise.

If you want to check that your HTML is valid, then the W3C guidelines would be best.

Where can we find them?

Moodle has made it very easy to check both HTML and accessibility, through services provided by the W3C and HiSoftware Cynthia Says (accessibility). All that you need to do is log in as an administrator, and then navigate to **Server | Debugging | Debug messages** and choose **NORMAL: Show errors, warnings and notices**, as seen below:

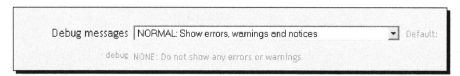

When this is done, at the bottom of every page, there will be a new set of links that when clicked, pass the page's details on to the relevant validators. Give it a go and see what happens.

Moodle for mobile devices

With the proliferation of mobile devices and PDAs loaded with fully-functional web browsers, Moodle has had to keep up with the times. There is a *Moodle for Mobile* that can be used with basic mobile phones and PDAs, but this lacks graphical elements and is therefore rather difficult to use.

The Orangewhitepda theme

There is also an *Orangewhitepda* theme that comes with the standard release of Moodle that can be used for mobile devices. This is a low-graphics, large-text theme that again can be customized fully to meet your requirements. The options here are to build a whole Moodle site specifically for mobile devices by using this theme, or to have a link somewhere on the front page of Moodle that loads this theme. To do this, you would need to use session themes, so that a particular theme is loaded for the users based upon the session.

How do we use it?

To do this, two things need to be done. Firstly, you will need to add the following PHP code to the `config.php` file in the root of your Moodle installation folder. That's right—not the other one in the root of your theme's folder.

```
$CFG->allowthemechangeonurl = true;
```

The `config.php` file is located at: `C:\Program Files\Apache Software Foundation\Apache2.2\htdocs\config.php`.

Once you have done this, you can then create a link to your *Moodle for Mobile* theme somewhere on your home page. When clicked, Moodle would load the *orangewhitepda* theme only for that session.

Adding a theme splash screen

You may have noticed that most themes have a splash screen when they are accessed for the first time. This screen is a useful way of conveying important information about the theme or your organization. Here is an example; in this case it is the *Autumn* theme by *Patrick Malley*:

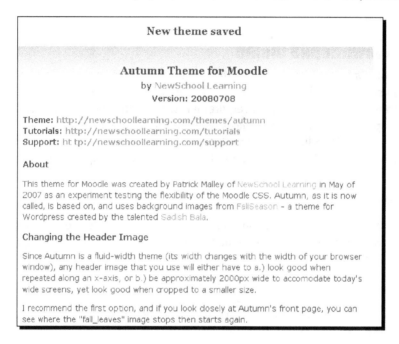

How do we do this?

All that we need to do to have a theme splash screen is to add an HTML file called `readme.html` in the theme's root folder. You can add any information that you want in this file, including links and graphics, if required.

Give it a go, and create a basic `readme.html` file. Enter the theme name into it, and then save this file to your theme's folder.

Obviously, you will probably want to add more information, and format the headers and links (if any) so that they are more prominent.

Adding a theme screenshot

Another thing that you have probably noticed when you have been selecting themes from your theme selector page is that all of the themes that load have a screenshot so that the administrator can see what the theme looks like. You will probably want to do this as well, not because the normal Moodle user will ever get to see this page but more as a way of making your theme complete. You might also have assigned other administrative users that need to be able to see this page and the themes that your Moodle site has installed.

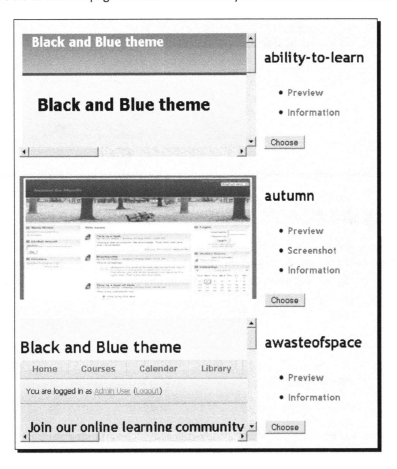

How do we add a theme screenshot?

Again, this is very easy to achieve, and only requires that you take a screenshot of your theme on its home page and then add this screenshot as a `.jpg` file into your theme's root folder. Try this out by pressing the *Print Screen* key on your keyboard and opening a new file in Adobe Photoshop. Paste in the screenshot from your clipboard and use the **Save for web & devices** menu in Photoshop. This will optimize the image at the same time as saving it, making it more accessible to people with slow Internet connections.

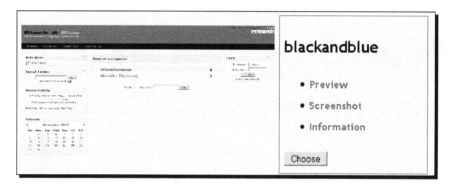

Changing the column order

The last enhancement that we are going to discuss is changing the column order in Moodle. There are times when you might need the default column order to be changed. You might, for instance, want both the left- and right-hand columns on one side of your theme, or want them loaded in a completely different order.

Left, right, and middle

To change the column order, you need to make sure that the theme's `config.php` file has the following settings added to it:

```
$THEME->layouttable = array('left', 'middle', 'right');

/// These values define the order of the columns for all
/// pages showing sideblocks. If not set Moodle uses the
/// default order:
/// $THEME->layouttable = array('left', 'middle', 'right');
```

Try this with the `left` and `right` together, and see what happens.

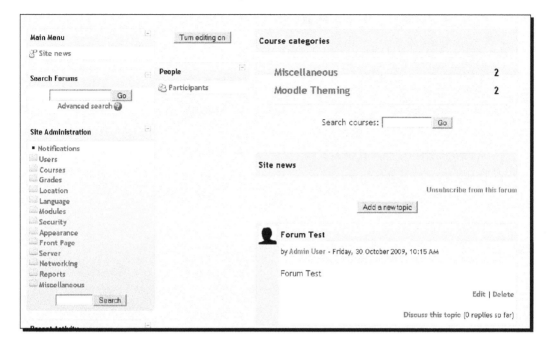

It's a little strange, but I have seen themes in the past that have used this technique very effectively.

Summary

In this chapter, we have been discussing some further enhancements that can be made to Moodle and to your Moodle theme. You have learned how to make some more CSS changes to make your theme even better, and have addressed some issues on the way. You have also learned why you should use the Moodle features demo course for testing purposes, and have looked at the reasons why you would create and use a Moodle course theme. Finally, we have discussed how to check your Moodle site with W3C validators, and have learned how to finish off our theme with a theme splash screen and theme selector image.

Specifically, we covered:

- Changing buttons and form fields
- Creating a CSS rollover and drop-down menus
- Consolidating CSS statements
- Downloading and installing the Moodle features demo
- Creating a course theme, and why we would do this
- Validating any HTML code that we have created
- Adding a theme splash screen and screenshot
- Changing the column order

B
Glossary of Useful Terms and Acronyms

Accessibility: Web accessibility refers to the practice of making websites usable by people of all abilities and disabilities. A variety of techniques, such as having high and low contrast color schemes, are used to ensure that people who have visual disabilities can still access the content.

Add-ons: Another term used for "extensions" in Mozilla Firefox, and is sometimes used as a term for Moodle plug-ins or modules.

Administration block: The block in Moodle that has the main administrative functions used to control the way that Moodle functions.

Adobe Photoshop: One of the world's leading graphic and photo manipulation software packages. For those who don't have the money or do not want to use proprietary software, there are open source alternatives such as GIMP. (Please see separate entry for GIMP later in this chapter.)

ALT tag: An alternative description tag for images in HTML. This will be displayed instead of the image if the user disables images in his or her browser.

Apache: A public, open source, web server software application.

Attribute: A value associated with an element, consisting of a name, and an associated value.

Blackboard: The largest of the commercial VLE competitors to Moodle.

Breadcrumb trail: A term used to provide a clear navigation route back to the home page of a website.

Browser: Any software used for "browsing" the Internet.

Browser compatibility: The concept that web pages should look similar in all browsers.

Class Selector: A syntax for specifying a CSS selector by using the class attribute of an element.

CSS: An abbreviation for Cascading Style Sheets—a technique of separating functionality from presentation.

Debugging: The process of checking computer code for errors.

Declaration: A matching pair of property and value parameters that creates a CSS style for a selector.

Design mockup: A sample design created with graphic manipulation software.

Dialog box: An instructional box that is used with software, including web browsers, to give instructions to users.

Drop-down menu: A menu system for websites and software packages that displays a menu of options when the user clicks on or hovers the mouse over the links or a predefined area.

Elements: Refers to each individual part of a web page. Elements can be blocks, boxes, navigational areas, or content sections that sometimes have CSS declarations associated with them.

Firebug: A Mozilla Firefox extension that allows the user to inspect HTML and CSS code.

Font: The typeface of text displayed on a computer.

Footer: The bottom section of a Moodle page.

GIMP: A free, open source, graphics manipulation software package.

Google Chrome: A web browser created by Google.

Grouped Selector: A means of grouping a range of selectors in a comma-separated list.

Header: The top section of a Moodle page.

HTML (Hypertext Markup Language): The main language used to create web pages.

HTML editor: A web-based text editor, normally present in web applications such as Moodle. This allows the user to have a **WYSIWYG (What You See Is What You Get)** editor experience.

Internet Explorer: A web browser created by Microsoft.

LAMP: A free, open source software stack consisting of Linux (OS), Apache (web server), MySQL (database), and PHP (scripting language).

Moodle: Acronym for **Modular Object-Oriented Dynamic Learning Environment**. Moodle is an open source course management system, originally developed by Martin Dougiamas. It is used by thousands of educational institutions around the world to provide an organized interface for e-learning or learning over the Internet.

Moodle docs: The Moodle documentation wiki where all of the Moodle documents are kept. (`http:moodle.org/docs`)

MySQL: The world's most popular open source database.

PDF (Portable Document Format): A document type created by Adobe specifically for the transfer and rendering of electronic documents regardless of the operating system being used.

PHP: A scripting language for producing dynamic web pages.

Platforms: A term used to refer to the type of operating system that an application runs on.

Rollover menu: A website menu that changes the color or style of either the background or font color when the user hovers his or her mouse over the links.

Safari: A web browser created by Apple Macintosh for Apple computers. It can now be run on Windows and Linux as well.

Screenshot: An exact captured image of the computer monitor's visible area.

Sideblock: The name for Moodle's content areas on either side (right and left) of the screen.

Slice and dice: The practice of slicing up a mockup graphic for use in a web page design.

Splash screen: The opening screen for software programs and websites.

Theme: Refers to the user "view" (interface) that can be chosen by the site administrator, teacher, or student (if enabled).

Theme priority: The order in which Moodle loads different themes.

Theme types: The different types of themes available to the Moodle application. These are site themes, user themes, course themes, category themes, session themes, and page themes.

User agent: A software application that is used to view web pages or electronic documents. It is typically a web browser.

Validators: Software systems that validate code against predefined rules. An HTML validator will check that the HTML code is valid by comparing it against the correct HTML rules.

WAMP: The Windows version of LAMP, consisting of Windows (OS), Apache (web server), MySQL (database), and PHP (scripting language).

Wireframe: A method used to visually map out the different areas of a website, or to map functionality.

WordPad: A compact Microsoft text editor with basic formatting capabilities for editing files that use the standard `.txt` file extension.

W3C: Acronym for **World Wide Web Consortium**. It is an international community that develops standards to ensure the long-term growth of the Web.

XML (Extensible Markup Language): Used to create standards-compliant content delivery.

Pop Quiz Answers

Chapter 2

Moodle Themes

1	To navigate to the **Theme Selector**, you need to go to **Appearance	Themes	Theme Selector**. So the correct answer is: **D**
2	To restrict a user from picking a theme from their profile, you should remove the unwanted themes from the **Theme list** in the **Theme settings** page. So the correct answer is: **A**
3	You have to use category themes with caution because it uses a lot of server overhead to traverse through all the different categories and sub-categories. The correct answer is therefore: **C**

Chapter 3

Customizing the Header and Footer

1	There are two pieces of title code in the `header.html` file because Moodle loads on the front page a different header from the inner pages. The correct answer is: **B**
2	To make a piece of code unused by Moodle, we would put a comment around it. So the answer is: **B**

3	The correct format to comment out code in a PHP file is:
	`/*my comment*/`
	It is called a comment because you can also use it to place inline comments inside PHP code blocks.
	So the correct answer is:
	C

Chapter 4

Adjusting the Colors and Fonts

1	We normally use WordPad instead of Notepad to edit HTML and PHP files because it retains most of the original formatting. So the answer is:
	C
	(There are other text editors of course, so please do use any text editor that you are used to.)
2	Mozilla Firefox is a great browser for Moodle themers because it looks good, it's quick to download, has hundreds of free extensions, and is free. So all of the answers are correct. Did you spot this? If you did, then well done!
3	If we need to change the style of a link when the mouse is rolled over it, then we need to change the `a:hover` CSS link selector. The answer is therefore:
	C

Chapter 5

Changing the Layout

1	The type of layout recommended for Moodle is a liquid layout. Of course, this is up to you but courses tend to better with a liquid layout. The answer is:
	A
2	The answer is:
	A
3	We need to take care when setting the sideblock widths and test these changes by installing other blocks, as some Moodle sideblocks have their width hardcoded directly in the block itself. And the sideblock width will also have an effect on how the course pages look. So the correct answers are:
	B and C

Index

M

Thank you for buying
Moodle 1.9 Theme Design Beginner's Guide

About Packt Publishing

Packt, pronounced 'packed', published its first book "*Mastering phpMyAdmin for Effective MySQL Management*" in April 2004 and subsequently continued to specialize in publishing highly focused books on specific technologies and solutions.

Our books and publications share the experiences of your fellow IT professionals in adapting and customizing today's systems, applications, and frameworks. Our solution based books give you the knowledge and power to customize the software and technologies you're using to get the job done. Packt books are more specific and less general than the IT books you have seen in the past. Our unique business model allows us to bring you more focused information, giving you more of what you need to know, and less of what you don't.

Packt is a modern, yet unique publishing company, which focuses on producing quality, cutting-edge books for communities of developers, administrators, and newbies alike. For more information, please visit our website: www.packtpub.com.

About Packt Open Source

In 2010, Packt launched two new brands, Packt Open Source and Packt Enterprise, in order to continue its focus on specialization. This book is part of the Packt Open Source brand, home to books published on software built around Open Source licences, and offering information to anybody from advanced developers to budding web designers. The Open Source brand also runs Packt's Open Source Royalty Scheme, by which Packt gives a royalty to each Open Source project about whose software a book is sold.

Writing for Packt

We welcome all inquiries from people who are interested in authoring. Book proposals should be sent to author@packtpub.com. If your book idea is still at an early stage and you would like to discuss it first before writing a formal book proposal, contact us; one of our commissioning editors will get in touch with you.

We're not just looking for published authors; if you have strong technical skills but no writing experience, our experienced editors can help you develop a writing career, or simply get some additional reward for your expertise.

Moodle 1.9 for Teaching 7-14 Year Olds: Beginner's Guide

ISBN: 978-1-847197-14-6   Paperback: 236 pages

Effective e-learning for younger students using Moodle as your Classroom Assistant

1. Focus on the unique needs of young learners to create a fun, interesting, interactive, and informative learning environment your students will want to go on day after day

2. Engage and motivate your students with games, quizzes, movies, and podcasts the whole class can participate in

3. Go paperless! Put your lessons online and grade them anywhere, anytime

Moodle Course Conversion: Beginner's Guide

ISBN: 978-1-847195-24-1   Paperback: 316 pages

Taking existing classes online quickly with the Moodle LMS

1. No need to start from scratch! This book shows you the quickest way to start using Moodle and e-learning, by bringing your existing lesson materials into Moodle.

2. Move your existing course notes, worksheets, and resources into Moodle quickly then improve your course, taking advantage of multimedia and collaboration.

3. Moving marking online â€" no more backbreaking boxes of assignments to lug to and from school or college.

Please check **www.PacktPub.com** for information on our titles

Moodle 1.9 E-Learning Course Development

ISBN: 978-1-847193-53-7   Paperback: 384 pages

A complete guide to successful learning
using Moodle

1. Updated for Moodle version 1.9

2. Straightforward coverage of installing and
   using the Moodle system

3. Working with Moodle features in all
   learning environments

4. A unique course-based approach focuses
   your attention on designing well-structured,
   interactive, and successful courses

Moodle 1.9 Teaching Techniques

ISBN: 978-1-849510-06-6   Paperback: 216 pages

Creative ways to build powerful and effective
online courses

1. Motivate students from all backgrounds,
   generations, and learning styles

2. When and how to apply the different learning
   solutions with workarounds, providing
   alternative solutions

3. Easy-to-follow, step-by-step instructions
   with screenshots and examples for Moodle's
   powerful features

4. Especially suitable for university and
   professional teachers

Moodle 1.9 Math

ISBN: 978-1-847196-44-6   Paperback: 276 pages

Integrate interactive math presentations, build feature-rich quizzes, set online quizzes and tests, incorporate Flash games, and monitor student progress using the Moodle e-learning platform

1. Get to grips with converting your mathematics teaching over to Moodle

2. Engage and motivate your students with exciting, interactive, and engaging online math courses with Moodle, which include mathematical notation, graphs, images, video, audio, and more

3. Integrate multimedia elements in math courses to make learning math interactive and fun

Moodle 1.9 Multimedia

ISBN: 978-1-847195-90-6   Paperback: 272 pages

Engaging online language learning activities using the Moodle platform

1. Ideas and best practices for teachers and trainers on using multimedia effectively in Moodle

2. Ample screenshots and clear explanations to facilitate learning

3. Covers working with TeacherTube, embedding interactive Flash games, podcasting, and more

4. Create instructional materials and design students' activities around multimedia

Please check **www.PacktPub.com** for information on our titles

Moodle 1.9 for Second Language Teaching

ISBN: 978-1-847196-24-8   Paperback: 524 pages

Engaging online language learning activities using the Moodle platform

1. A recipe book for creating language activities using Moodle 1.9

2. Get the most out of Moodle 1.9's features to create enjoyable, useful language learning activities

3. Create an online language learning centre that includes reading, writing, speaking, listening, vocabulary, and grammar activities

Moodle Administration

ISBN: 978-1-847195-62-3   Paperback: 376 pages

An administrator's guide to configuring, securing, customizing, and extending Moodle

1. A complete guide for planning, installing, optimizing, customizing, and configuring Moodle

2. Secure, back up, and restore your VLE

3. Extending and networking Moodle

4. Detailed walkthroughs and expert advice on best practices